CARNATION

Reaktion's Botanical series is the first of its kind, integrating horticultural and botanical writing with a broader account of the cultural and social impact of trees, plants and flowers.

CARNATION

Twigs Way

REAKTION BOOKS

This book is dedicated to our very own 'Carnation, Lily, Lily, Rose'

Published by
REAKTION BOOKS LTD
Unit 32, Waterside
44–48 Wharf Road
London N1 7UX, UK

www.reaktionbooks.co.uk

First published 2016

Printed and bound in China by 1010 Printing International Ltd

A catalogue record for this book is available from the British Library

ISBN 978 1 78023 634 6

Contents

Dianthus caryophyllus, from the *Florilegium* of Alexander Marshal (*c.* 1620–1682).

one

The Divine Flower

What shall I say to the Queene of delight and of flowers, Carnations and Gilloflowers, whose bravery, variety and sweete smell joined together, tyeth every one's affection with great earnestnesse both to like and to have them?

JOHN PARKINSON, *Paradisi in sole, paradisus terrestris* (1629)

After women, flowers are the most divine creations.

CHRISTIAN DIOR, couturier and perfumier

It all starts with a name: *Dios anthus: Dios* from the Greek for Zeus, the chief god of the Olympians, and *anthos* from flower. Thus flower of god. The philosopher and naturalist Theophrastus (*c.* 371–288 BC), known as the 'Father of Botany', was the first to describe and name the plant, setting it on its journey through time and space. Why the Greeks should have chosen the small wild carnation above all other flowers upon which to bestow divinity can only be guessed, but the name stuck with only very slight alteration to create the Latin nomenclature of *Dianthus*. After that the continuity of naming is rather spoilt by the fact that no one knows for certain exactly which of the many wild pink coloured flowers of the dianthus family the Greeks had originally been referring to. In fact over three hundred species of plants are now known to inhabit this blessed genus, ranging from the tiny Alpine pinks of central Europe to the tall exuberant *Dianthus superbus* that spreads its deeply cut petals from Norway to Japan. The wild carnation most likely to have been observed by Theophrastus is the *Dianthus sylvestris* and do not appear to modern eyes to have been especially marked for divinity, being shortish, half-hardy plants with thin pale leaves and single blooms of five petals in a light pink colour.[1] Given its natural blooming period of June to August it would have been easy to overlook the delicate, scentless plant and its single bloom in favour of the more boisterous and taller flowers of the summer months.

Mythology links the carnation not just to the Greek god Zeus but to the Roman goddess Diana, the goddess of the hunt and daughter of Zeus' Roman equivalent Jupiter. Taking human form to visit earth one day, as all gods and goddesses traditionally did, Diana is said to have come upon a shepherd boy and taken a liking to him. However, the youth turned down her advances, never a wise thing to do to a woman or a goddess, and in retaliation Diana ripped out his eyes and threw them to the ground. The eyes immediately sprouted and flowered and became the first 'Dianthus', which slightly puts one off the otherwise attractive flower.

The true 'carnation' (*Dianthus caryophyllus*), which is so familiar in our gardens and glasshouses, owes its second name to the spicy clove, the *Caryophyllus aromaticus* which so many of the carnation family imitate in their scent. 'Cary' refers to the nut of the clove plant, although to clear up any confusion with the carnation *Dianthus caryophyllus*, botanists have carefully reclassified the clove plant first as *Eugenia aromatica* and then as *Syzygium aromaticum*, leaving the carnation somewhat bereft.

Our earliest image of the dianthus of classical times comes from the ill-fated Roman town of Pompeii where a single flowered wild carnation (most likely *Dianthus sylvestris*) was depicted in a fresco. Topped by a goldfinch who is shown bending the slender stalk, the painting decorated the wall of what is now known as 'The House of the Faun'. The fragile image survived the devastation and destruction of the Vesuvian eruption of AD 79 but was sadly lost to the vagaries of the weather after being uncovered and recorded by archaeologists centuries later.[2] Pliny the Elder, who died in the same eruption that

Sydenham Teast Edwards, *Dianthus caryophyllus*, 'Wheatear carnation', 1813, watercolour.

preserved the fresco, had devoted much of his life to natural science and botany, producing a 37-volume work called *Natural History*. In it he described a pink or carnation known in southern Spain, referring to it by the name of 'Cantabrica', thereby adding confusion to the origins and naming of the flower when it came to be considered by sixteenth-century herbalists.

Spreading through Europe and Turkey with the crusaders of the Holy War, the wild carnation, or clove pink, made its home in the walls of French and English castles. The plant lover Henry Nicholson

Ellacombe (1822–1916) recorded in 1874 the traditional pink flower covering the old castle of Falaise in which William the Conqueror was born, and he mused on its long association with the warm, cream-coloured Caen stone. Ellacombe also observed it holding onto the stones of castle ruins in England at Dover, Deal, Rochester and Cardiff.[3] He believed it had been introduced 'by the Norman builders, perhaps, as a pleasant memory of their Norman houses', or perhaps accidentally brought in with the stones of which parts of the houses are built'.[4] Ellacombe noted in his diaries that the Conqueror himself, or his follower Guthlac, may have actually brought plants or seeds of the plant from France, as Ellacombe himself did, transferring seeds from Falaise Castle to his own vicarage gardens in Bitton, Gloucestershire.[5] The smaller Cheddar pink (*Dianthus caesius*, also known as *D. gratianopolitanus*) also thrived on Ellacombe's 'high south wall' in the gardens at Bitton, while at another house in the same village it was said to hang down 'in a beautiful mat, more than five

The Cheddar pink, *Dianthus gratianopolitanus*.

Grey-green foliage is a distinctive feature of the carnation and pink.

feet in length and three feet across'.[6] Long before it was the pride of a Bitton villager, a small pink (although it is not recorded which sort) could be seen in the London gardens of Henry de Lacy, Earl of Lincoln. Lacy's gardens at Holborn were said to be substantial, and included stew ponds and vineyards dating from the period when the palace had belonged to the Dominicans, giving us another early record of the pink's arrival and a suitably divine connection.[7]

Tracing the path of the dianthus through Europe is fraught with difficulties because early botanists invented new names for the same plant and gave the same name to different species. In 1597 John Gerard attempted to trace the 'diverse pinks' through the pages of previous herbalists, listing it as being identified as *Cantabrica* and *Stactice* by Pliny the Elder and William Turner (1508–1568), *Vetonica altera* and *Vetonica altilis* according to Rembert Dodoens in his herbal of 1554, and *Superba* by Gerard's friend Matthew L'Obel. To add to the muddle, the carnation, which by the late sixteenth century was clearly differentiated from the pink, had according to Gerard been confused with it by some earlier writers. His contemporaries knew it as the *Caryophyllus flos*, from where we later derived 'gariofilium', or 'gilofera' for short, and the sixteenth-century German botanist Leonhart Fuchs included the carnation in his *De historia stirpium*, with a wonderful engraving of a red- and white-flowered pot carnation labelled 'Caryophyllea'; but others thought it to be the same as the *Ocullus damascenus* or *Ocullus barbaricus* of ancient herbals. Some argued that it could be identified in the ancient writers as *Herba tunica* or *polemonia*, while the French physician and botanist Jean Ruel (1474–1537) thought that the 'ancients' did not know the carnation at all, being only familiar with its smaller cousins the pinks.[8] It is no wonder that the modern carnation specialist and writer Steven Bailey declared: 'The true origin of the border carnation is not altogether clear. Having researched in text books of years gone by, I still find the facts very confusing.'[9]

In the late thirteenth century the carnation is believed to have made it into southern Europe, hot on the heels of the pinks that had already marched into France and England. The year 1270 saw the divine flower in Tunis supposedly helping ease the sufferings of the troops of Louis IX under the boiling sun with their soothing

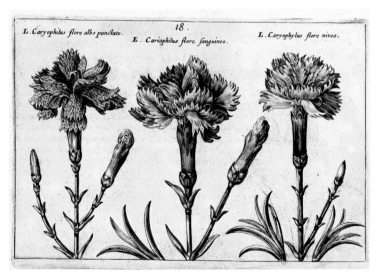

These exquisitely depicted carnations are over 400 years old, from Crispijn van de Passe, *Hortus Floridus* (1614).

qualities.[10] In his late fourteenth-century work *The Canterbury Tales*, the poet Chaucer recorded a fictional garden where: 'There springen herbes, grete and smale; The licoris and the set-ewale, And many a cloue gelofre and notemuge to put in ale, Whether it be moist or stale'.[11] Normally the 'clove gilloflower', or 'gillofre', would be taken to mean the carnation, gillofre being its common English name at this period, but some historians argue that the inclusion of such exotics as liquorice and nutmeg in Chaucer's list makes it more likely that he meant the real clove rather than its paler imitation. After six hundred years it is difficult to interpret the meaning of a poet and so a fourteenth-century arrival in England cannot be confirmed.[12] 'Gillyvore', 'gilofre' or 'gelofre' are all old English variations on what by the late seventeenth century was almost always referred to as the 'gillyflower'. Although often assumed to be a corruption of 'July flower', this may in fact derive from a corruption of the Latin term 'carophyllum', or clove. Thus Chaucer's reference to the 'clow-gelofre' would technically be tautological – 'clove clove' – but then medieval Latin/English could often produce these double takes, ensuring that both peasant and scholar knew what they were talking about. By 1460 the carnation was being grown under yet another name in the area around Valencia in Spain, and in Italy an illustration from Bocaccio's *La Teseída* (1460) depicts an enclosed garden or *hortus conclusus* with turf seats, a rose-covered trellis and pinks in the border. The distinctive pink and white dianthus were then newly arrived plants – so rare and precious in this elite castle garden.[13]

In the 1470s we see the first use of the term 'oeillet' in France that would later come to mean the carnation proper rather than the pink. Heading further north, a Flemish book of hours not only confirms the carnation's presence in northern Europe by 1500, but brings us back again to the divinity with which it is associated. In the margins of this particular work the carnation attains a giant size, straddling the lower part of the page and balanced precariously on a wheelbarrow, while the upper part of the page depicts a person at prayer.[14] Books of hours, exquisitely illuminated religious status

Page from a Flemish book of hours with Psalm 6 'Domine, ne in furore tuo' (O Lord, rebuke me not in your anger). The top left-hand corner depicts 'King David'; in the border is a woman with wheelbarrow, carnations, other flowers and butterflies.

symbols of the courtly elite throughout Europe, were strewn with carnations and pinks. Trailing along the borders or pictured in the miniature worlds, they echoed the religious texts, symbolizing variously the Passion and the love of God. White carnations represented female saints, while red flowers stood for the Passion, accompanying pea flowers symbolizing resurrection, strawberry plants purity and the Passion, and the columbine the Holy Spirit. Glimpses into tiny jewelled gardens might include images of pots of carnations, constrained by the typical trellis or woven work of the period, keeping the flower heads upright. In the prayer book of Juana of Castile (illustrated by Gheraert David in *c.* 1498), three pots of carnations standing stiffly within their woven cages are placed within a flower border below the window which itself contains a pot of Madonna lilies.[15] Carnations might also take on the symbolism of the grander and more voluptuous rose, itself symbolic of divine love. Pinks and carnations are also seen in window pots and along borders in the painting by Dieric Bouts created around 1490 for Isabella of Spain, where the Madonna and saints watch over the Christ Child while reading their own books of hours and inhabiting the world of the fifteenth century.[16]

Most famously the Renaissance master Raffaello Sanzia da Urbino (better known as Raphael) included the small innocent pink in his painting *Madonna of the Pinks* (*c.* 1506–7). A youthful Virgin Mary holds a small posy of pinks in one hand while the Christ Child on her lap playfully takes two in his own hand. The image draws not just on the divine naming of the pink (in this case probably the diminutive *Dianthus plumaris*), but on one of a complex web of Christian symbols that had attached themselves to the plant by this period. The delicate pink flower of the dianthus, although no one knows which one, was said to have first appeared where the tears of the Virgin Mary fell at the base of the cross, becoming a symbol of mother's love as well as of the Crucifixion itself.[17] It was in this guise of the love of Mary that pinks and later carnations appeared in churches at Easter, sometimes being scattered or placed in small

Detail of Vittore
Carpaccio, *The Dream
of St Ursula*, 1495,
tempera on canvas.

posies under depictions of the Mother of God, a connection which
survives today through its association with Mother's Day in the u.s.,
where carnations are given to mothers and appear on numerous
Mother's Day cards. The dianthus was often seen in the hand of the
Virgin Mary or Christ in paintings and Raphael's depiction was by
no means unusual in the fifteenth century. In Andrea Mantegna's
Madonna of Victory, 1496 (in the Louvre), the Christ Child is again
pictured with his mother, holding two carnations, possibly symbolizing his dual nature of divine and human – or perhaps his present
and his future? The cryptically named artist 'Follower of the Master
of the St Ursula Legend' created a scene of surprising informality
with the same components.

Soon the dianthus, and more particularly the clove carnation,
became associated with the Passion in other ways. The clove-like

Carlo Crivelli, *Virgin and Child*, c. 1480, tempera on panel.
The carnation is used as a religious symbol.

smell of the pink, and its association with gillyvore (also derived
from the Arabic *quaranful* or later *karanfil*), brought to medieval minds
the shape of the clove itself, resembling the wooden nails used to nail
Christ to the Cross – the Clavos de Cristo of the Spanish, who coincidentally boast the carnation as their national flower. This association
was also recorded in Italy, where the flower was commonly called

Follower of the Master of the St Ursula Legend (Bruges).
The Virgin and Child with Two Angels, c. 1490. The Virgin is seated
before a cloth of honour and holds a carnation or pink.

chiodino (little nail) because of the shape of its buds, and thus became
again associated with the Passion of Christ.[18] In Russia the term
gvozdika is also used for both the pink and the carnation, sharing an
etymological root with *gvozd* (гвоздь) meaning hobnail, nail or pin.
'Incarnation' was also used as an alternative version of the flower

name 'coronation' or 'carnation' in the sixteenth and seventeenth centuries in England, giving a more direct link to the Passion in an era when coincidence of language was an important part of belief. William Turner (1508–1568), the naturalist who produced his own herbal in 1551, 1562 and 1568, is among those who refer to the carnation as the 'Incarnacyon'.[19] Sharing a name with a fundamental doctrine of Christianity, that the Son of God became flesh, soon led to other attributes of the small flower playing a multiplicity of roles in Christian belief and art.

Pentecost, fifty days after the time of the Crucifixion on Good Friday, was often celebrated in northern European churches and homes by bringing the carnation or, more probably, the pink, into churches. Known as *Pfingsten* in Germany, the celebration of Pentecost marks the coming of the Holy Spirit and coincidentally is the start of the plethora of early summer blooms for many European countries, including those of some species of dianthus. Indeed the inclusion of the element 'pink' in 'pinks' has been claimed by some writers to derive from this flowering at the time of the 'Pfingsten' or 'pinksten', although a more likely explanation comes from the pinking or cutting of the petal edges.

From the Virgin as Mother of Christ and symbol of mother's love, the same flower soon made the leap to symbol of marriage through Mary's role as Bride of Christ and from marriage back to love, both secular and religious. With so many meanings to choose from, the interpretation of religious and secular art of the fifteenth century onwards presents difficulties. The popular subject of Madonna and Christ Child may thus be claimed to represent the love between mother and child or Mary as Bride of Christ, or, more darkly, presage Christ's ultimate fate.

When included in fifteenth- and sixteenth-century portraits of less divine mortals, the dianthus also has variable meanings depending on the role of the sitter and the understanding of the artist, factors which modern observers may not be privy to. *Portrait of Man with Carnation* by the Netherlandish painter Jan van Eyck is most

Mother's Day is associated with carnations across the world, as depicted in this vintage postcard from the 1920s.

likely to include the single dianthus to indicate the man's religious thoughts as the sitter is also wearing a prominent cross indicating the Order of St Anthony.[20] *Portrait of a Man with a Pink Carnation* (c. 1475) by Hans Memling also shows a man with clerical dress holding a single flower.[21] However, a self-portrait by the artist Michael Ostendorfer (c. 1520?) depicts the artist in all his finery of furs and linen and a later reference records the full title as *Self-portrait as Bridegroom*. Here, then, the dianthus is most likely used in its meaning of earthly love.[22] Women with carnations may also be seen as either worldly or religious and the viewer depends on other indications, such as a hand on a Bible (the portrait of Anna Goch c. 1647, *Portrait of a Woman with Ruff, Hat, Veil, a Red Carnation and a Book*), to indicate which is meant. The 1519 portrait of the Duchess of Gelders provides us with one of our earliest secular portraits of a woman with a carnation, and rather delightfully includes a small pot with three carnation blossoms as well as the one she holds. Pairs of portraits may depict engaged lovers, a bride and groom, or an older couple content in their marriage. Rembrandt's *Woman with a Pink* shows just such a woman in a markedly sombre frame of mind, despite holding her carnation aloft and being dressed in the best finery of a secular married woman.[23] The 1542 portrait in which the English prince, later Edward VI, is variously cited as holding a carnation or a rose is a sign of how similar the flattened wilder roses of the Tudor period were to the multi-petalled

Portrait of the Duchess of Gelders, holding a carnation and wearing a plumed hat, *c.* 1500–1550, woodcut with hand colouring.

Renaissance tin-glazed earthenware known as *belle donne* (beautiful women):
these Renaissance plates have usually been interpreted as tokens of love
relating to courtship and marriage.

carnation. In fact, the merits and similarities of the two were often
debated by later florists, both being highly scented summer flowers
beloved by gardeners and flower collectors of all social ranks.

By the sixteenth century a close relation of the carnation, the
little Carthusian pink (*Dianthus carthusianorum*), was marching across
Europe side by side with the spread of the Carthusian monks from
whom it took its name. At the great monastery Grande Chartreuse,
founded in 1084 in the Chartreuse mountains near Grenoble, the
Carthusians were great gardeners and apothecaries, and each monk
had his own separate garden adjoining his cell in which many grew
the small brightly coloured pink. At home on its native limestone
hillsides in southern and central Europe, the pink had been brought

to England by the Carthusians by 1573, although its small clustered flowers on short alpine stems never caught on in the same way as its larger cousins. While the Carthusian pink grew in monastic gardens and on steep mountainsides, in the sixteenth century it was believed that the carnation had grown in the Garden of Eden and appears there not only in paintings of the period but also in the allegorical frontispiece to John Parkinson's 1629 history of plants, *Paradisi in sole, paradisus terrestris*. Standing proudly next to a miniature Adam, the carnation overtops a martagon lily and a strange prickly pear as well

Carthusian pink, *Dianthus carthusianorum*, so called owing to its association with Carthusian monks.

as keeping company with plants newly introduced into Europe, such as the pineapple. New to Europe they might be, reasoned Parkinson, but they were part of God's great design and had thus been present since his Creation. Barnaby Googe, a late sixteenth-century writer and friend of the great 'gardener' statesman William Cecil, combined a reference to the biblical past of the carnation with a new take on the 'July' flower: 'Oh what sweete and goodly Gely floures are here, you may truely say that Solomon in all his princely pompe was never able to attayne to this beautie.' The scent was also said to address the 'spirituall parts' and keep them from 'terrible and fearful dreames through their heavenly savour and moste sweet pleasant odour'.[24]

This mix of divinity, spirituality, sexuality and symbolism is rife in the medieval tale of *Roman de la Rose* (Romance of the Rose), one of the most popular and widely retold prose poems in the Renaissance period. An extended allegory, originally by Guillaume de Lorris (*c.* 1230), the poem recounted the stages of a courtly love affair. In brief, a chivalric lover hunts for the rosebud that represents his heart's desire. After long searches he is let into the walled garden of love by a lady representing idleness, where he finally locates the rose, which symbolizes both love and lust. The tale's numerous editions and additions, including a substantial rewrite by Chaucer, gave plentiful opportunity for a choice of flowers in the illustration of this paradis-iacal garden. A fifteenth-century copy contains exquisite illustrations of the interior of the walled garden of love, featuring a border packed with carnations standing proudly by the warm wall. Whether these were in the mind of Chaucer or added by an independently minded illustrator, their spicy scents and symbolism of betrothal would have made them a perfect choice for such a setting. Dianthus appear again in the Renaissance romance of Renaud de Montauban where, in a fifteenth-century version, the lovers Maugis and la belle Oriande are pictured sitting on a bench with a large pot of carnations next to them, perhaps hinting at a betrothal.[25] Held in the Arsenal Library in Paris, the illustration is one of the most touching portrayals of lovers, reaching down the centuries to modern valentines.

Admiration of the carnation was not restricted to Christians. In the Ottoman culture the carnation, or *karanfil*, was one of the four most important flowers in the gardens of paradise alongside the rose, hyacinth and tulip. The *karanfil* was both a symbol of life and the source of life. This role gave to the carnation a divine inner beauty that was said to evoke spiritual contemplation and is the reason for its inclusion on pottery and embroidery. Depending on whether the context was a spiritual or an earthly one, the quartet of flowers might together represent aspects of love and sexuality, or aspects of the divine. Outdoor social gatherings were a fundamental part of Ottoman culture, and weddings, dinners and circumcision feasts were all held in enclosed private gardens filled with jewel-like flower beds and central water pools. In the works of the poet Revani (d. 1524), garden and guests were both praised in terms of flowers:

> Whoever wants a party in the rose garden
> let him have a private sohbet
> With a beloved whose hair is a hyacinth
> whose face is a rose, lips a bud.

Visiting Isfahan in Persia in the mid-seventeenth century, the Anglo-French traveller Sir John Chardin recorded that the gardens and wild meadows contained 'a most unusual flower called the clove pink, each plant bearing some thirty blooms', as well as the normal pinks which could be seen in gardens and in the Persian miniatures of the period.[26]

Persian culture overflows with poems where the beloved is almost subsumed beneath allegory. The face of the beloved is a garden, the cheeks a rose or pomegranate flower, the chin an apple or quince, the lips a bud or pomegranate seed, the eye an almond, the locks of hair a hyacinth. Rather than suggesting an individual feature, the carnation through its extended blooming period represented the everlasting nature of love. The traveller Lady Mary Wortley Montagu, who accompanied her husband on his ambassadorship

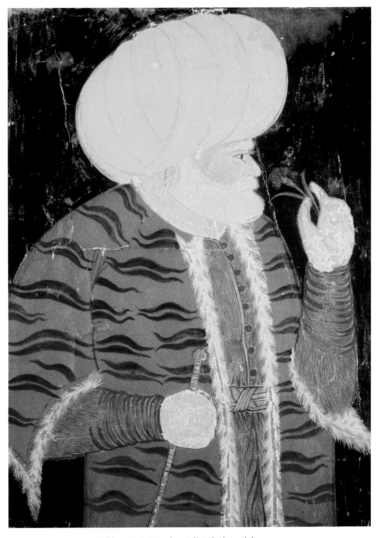

Nakkep Reis Haydar, *Admiral Khair-ed-din*, 1540.

to Istanbul in the early eighteenth century, recorded the meanings of colours, flowers and fruits at that time through her access to the women of the court harem. The carnation was recorded as meaning, among other things, 'I have long lov'd you and you have not known it.' Long-lasting blooms also turned the carnation into a political symbol of a powerful ruler, although perhaps one with a penchant

İznik tile with carnation between hyacinths, 17th century.

for gardens and scent with a hint of romance. Admiral Khair-ed-din, 'Barbarossa', a grand admiral during the reign of Suleiman the Magnificent (1520–66), had his portrait painted while holding a carnation to his nose. Barbarossa's portrait is very similar in style to that of the Sultan Mehmet II, the distinction being that Mehmet was shown holding a rose to his nose.[27]

Carnations also appeared on ceramics and tiles used in the decoration of elite Ottoman residences and religious buildings. Centred on the İznik region, these high-quality wares of the fifteenth and, most particularly, sixteenth century included the floral repertoire of *sukufe* which can still be seen on the palaces of Istanbul, the mosque of Rüstem Pasa (*c.* 1561) and the mausoleums of Roxelane (1558) and Suleiman the Magnificent (1566). The use of such designs across

Iranian prayer mat with border of red carnations, c. 1800–1860.

Turkey and into Syria brought another religious association to the carnation. The distinctive, fanlike arrangement of flower petals was to be depicted on walls of some of the most important religious monuments across Turkey, from Constantinople, with one foot in Europe, to Damascus and Aleppo, and across into Persia (Iran), the heartland of Islam. The divine carnation knew no bounds.

two

What's in a Name?

❧

Let yon admired Carnation own
Not all was meant for raiment or for food,
Not all for needful use alone;
There while the seeds of future blossoms dwell,
'Tis coloured for the sight, perfumed to please the smell.

WILLIAM SHENSTONE (1714–1763), poet and garden writer

Already burdened with the names *dianthus* in Greek, *oeillets* in French, *clavel* in Spanish, *garofoli* in Italian and *quaranfil* in Persian, once the carnation and pink reached English shores they were christened with a plethora of 'common names' by those for whom Greek and Latin or the languages of mainland Europe were a distant irrelevance. These names were in turn duly recorded by the herbalist and botanists of the day, alongside the confusion of classical sources, before making their way into popular culture in the form of recipes, garden books, love songs and plays. For the carnation the most common names were 'gilloflower', 'blunket', 'horseflesh', 'clove gilloflower' and 'sops-in-wine', with 'coronation', 'carnation' or 'incarnation' following on. John Gerard attempted to list all the common names at the end of the sixteenth century, including 'some whereof are called Carnations, others Clove Gillflowers, some Sops in wine, some Pagients or Pagion colour, Horseflesh, blunket, purple, white, double and single Gilloflowers, as also a Gilloflower with yellow flowers', also 'Sweet Johns and

Czechoslovakian stamp, c. 1979, depicting the graceful but hardy *Dianthus glacialis*.

Sweet Williams and sundrie Pinks'. The 'wild gilloflower, jagged pinks, mountain pinks, Cheddar pinks and Deptford pinks along with virginal or maidenly pinks', were known by Gerard as different varieties – but all could be commonly referred to simply as 'pinkes' or 'small honesties'.

Of these common and popular names some are easier to account for than others: pink and pinks are perhaps the most misleading. Henry Lyte in his English translation of *Nievve herball*, 1578, refers to the 'pynkes and small feathered Gillofers' as 'like to the double or cloave Gillofers in leaves, stalkes and floures, saving they be single and a great deal smaller', but remarks of their flower, 'like to the Gillofers aforesayde, saving each floure is single with five or six small leaves, deepe and finely snipt, or frenged like to small feathers'.[1] John Parkinson also referred to the flower of a particular nectarine plant with an indented petal as being 'with a pincking blossom'. It was this fringing or pinking, done to stop fabric fraying, rather than

The 1578 English translation by Henry Lyte of Rembert Dodoens's *Nievve herball* (or the History of Plants) refers to 'Gillofers'.

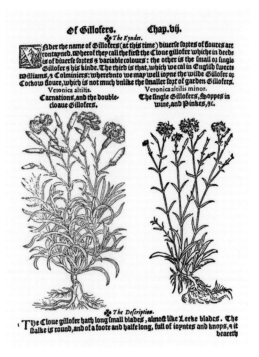

Of Gillofers. **Chap. bij.**

The Kyndes.

Nder the name of Gillofers (at this time) diuerse sortes of floures are contayned, wherof they call the first the Cloue gillofer whiche in deede is of diuerse sortes & variable colours: the other is the small or single Gillofer & his kinde. The third is that, which we call in English sweete williams, & Colminiers: wherebnto we may well ioyne the wilde Gillofer or Cockow floure, which is not much vnlike the smaller sort of garden Gillofers.

Vetonica altilis. Carnations, and the double cloue Gillofers.

Vetonica altilis minor. The single Gillofers, Soppes in wine, and Pinkes, &c.

The Description.

The Cloue gillofer hath long small blades, almost like Leeke blades. The stalke is round, and of a foote and halfe long, full of ioyntes and knops, & it beareth

the colour, that was the generally accepted inspiration for the 'pink' until the contradictory 'smooth edged' pink was developed in the late eighteenth century. The pretty pink with jagged leaves is also referred to by Hugh Platt in 1575, in his *The Floures of Philosophies with the Pleasures of Poetrie*:

> Wherein the sweet carnations
> with roses do abounde.
> Here springs the goodly gelofers,
> some white, some redde in showe;
> Here prettie pinkes with jagged leaves
> on rugged rootes do growe.

Several years ago the vigorous single-flowered 'Purple' and 'White Jagged Pinks' of Gerard's *Herball* were discovered in a cemetery in Sussex County, Delaware, and these plus the 'Old Fringed White'

PINK
(DIANTHUS PLUMARIUS)
³/₄ Nat. size

PL. 38

Dianthus plumarius, the common pink, from Edward Step, *Favourite Flowers of the Garden and Greenhouse* (1897).

and 'Old Fringed Pink' were most probably those the plant-loving American president Thomas Jefferson was referring to when he recorded pinks blooming at Shadwell in 1767, or the planting of pinks at Poplar Forest, Virginia, in 1811.[2]

The oddest of the common names, 'horseflesh', perhaps refers to the most common colour of the flower, dating to the period before the plant itself had given rise to the use of the term 'pink' for a colour. This may also have resulted in 'blunket' – steed or horse in the Scottish dialect – although an alternative would be from the French *blanc* or *blanquet*, meaning white or light grey. The rather more mysterious 'sops-in-wine', generally thought to refer to the red clove gillyflower, may be explained by its inclusion in a fifteenth-century list of 'herbes for the copp [cup]', which suggests that the spicy flower was used to flavour the often rather rough wines. Whether the flowers themselves were the 'sops' or whether it referred to bread that was traditionally dipped into the flavoured wine is debated by scholars and might perhaps form the basis for a practical research project. A rather less culinary explanation could be that the stamens appearing within the centre of the dark red petals themselves looked like bread floating in wine. The modern 'sops in wine' is variously defined by nurseries as either red or white. In 1573 Thomas Tusser used the name 'sops-in-wine' in his list of flowers suited to the care of the country housewife in his *Five Hundred Good Points of Husbandrie*, where he makes it clear that the garden is the responsibility of the goodly housewife rather than the husband. Filling the pot, creating flavourings, concocting medicines and distilling scents were part of the housewife's duties and the carnation would appear in many of those duties.[3] The first garden book written specifically for women was by the Yorkshire vicar William Lawson in 1618, as part of his *A New Orchard and Garden*, entitled *The Country Housewife's Garden*. This small book within a book included a list of flowers suitable for such a garden, such as the 'Gilly flower' or the 'Clove flower'. Lawson preferred the clove carnation of the two:

The famous Allwoods Nursery include a white-petalled 'sops in wine' in their stock of Heritage Garden Pinks. Other nurseries use the same name for red-petalled forms with white splashes.

> I may well call them the King of flowers except the Rose,
> and the best sort of them are called Queen July-flowers.
> I have of them nine or ten several colours and divers of
> them as big as Roses, of all flowers (save the Damask Rose)
> they are the most pleasant in sight and smell.[4]

It is no wonder that in portraits of the period it can be difficult to distinguish between a small rose and a large carnation.

'Coronation', a favourite term of herbalists in the mid-sixteenth century, came perhaps from its use in chaplets, although the reference to a crown was thought by Henry Lyte, an English botanist and antiquary, to derive again from the ragged edging which 'the flowers dented, or toothed above – like to a littell crownet'.[5] 'Coronation' was also the version favoured by the poet Edmund Spenser in his *The Shepheardes Calender* of 1579, where he calls on his pastoral maids to 'Bring hither the pink and purple columbine with gilliflowers; Bring coronations and soppes-in-wine, worn of paramours' such that the entire dianthus family appears to do court to Queen Elizabeth (for whom the term 'coronation' would be suited). A courtly garden would be expected to provide the flowers for the queen's favour, as John Lyly (c. 1553–1606) describes in *Euphues and his England* (c. 1580), where a courtly Elizabethan garden contains

> what floure like you best in all this border, heere be faire Roses sweete Violets, fragrant Primroses. Heere will be Jilly-floures, carnations, sops in wine, sweet Johns and what may either please you for sight or delight you with savour.

By naming the jilly or gilliflower, as well as carnations and sops-in-wine, Spenser and Lyly confirm to us that they considered these names to denote for different flowers rather than being a variety of names for one,[6] although their fellow poet Michael Drayton (1563–1631) rather confuses the issue by referring, in his poem 'Poly-Olbion', to 'The brave carnation then, with sweet and sovereign power; So of his colour called although a July flower'. The 'colour called' referred of course to the flesh colour of the flower, of which 'carnation' links to the Latin *carnis*, or flesh, and takes us back to horseflesh and possibly blunket in a merry-go-round of naming.

The derivation of the gilliflower, gillyver or July flower has already been mentioned in Chapter One, along with the uncertainty as to whether it relates to the time of flowering, the clove scent or the original Arabic name, although given that the cast of summer flowers in England included the dame gillyflower (*Hesperis matronalis*, now often referred to as dame's violet), the wall gillyflower (the wallflower or *Cheiranthus cheiri*) and the mock gillyflower (soapwort or 'bouncing bet'), among a host of others, the derivation from the month of flowering would seem most probable. 'Williams', incidentally, were not as one might think the sweet william that we now know, itself a dianthus (*Dianthus barbatus*), but were in fact the wild 'crowflower', most probably a variation on *Lychnis flos-cuculi*, or ragged robin, which does look remarkably like a cross between a deeply indented wild pink and a tall sweet william and is at least a member of the Caryophyllaceae family. The garden historian Mark Griffiths has suggested that William Cecil, Lord Burghley, is holding a bunch of 'williams' on the frontispiece of Gerard's 1597 *Herball, or General Historie of Plants*.

Having spent their formative years in a plethora of naming indecisions, the most popular dianthus appear to have settled down by the early seventeenth century to the common English names that we still know them by three and a half centuries later – carnation, pink and sweet william – although cottagers still referred to the 'gilly-flower' well into the nineteenth century. Before the loss of such a wealth of confusion could be fully mourned, the striped, streaked and marbled varieties that were pouring out of the nurseries and florists' gardens took the mantle of romance and mystery upon themselves. A litany of varietal or cultivar names runs through John Parkinson's (1567–1650) work *Paradisi in sole, paradisus terrestris* of 1629, fascinating the curious gardener and historian alike. Who could resist the 'Bleeding Swain', the 'Whole Podder' or 'Lustie Gallant', and who had ruffled the 'Ruffling Robin'? So many fancy new carnation varieties were available that Parkinson and his fellow botanists used the term 'Old' for the plainer originals. The 'Old English Carnation' or 'Great Harwich' was one of Parkinson's favourites, along with the plain 'Clove Gilliflower' and the white carnation 'Delicate' – the latter of which he describes as 'a goodly delightful fair flower'. Those that appeared to derive from the 'Old English' or 'Harwich' carnation boasted names that began (in Latin) with *Caryophyllus maximus* and proceeded through a long addendum of descriptive naming that make the garden historian long for the advent of Carl Linnaeus and his binomial naming system of the 1760s. The *Caryophyllus maximus dictus Hulo ceruleo pupureus*, for example, was, as its name implied, a version of the old English carnation called the *hulo*, in which the large flower was of a fair purple colour curiously marbled with white but with the marbling so small that the flower appeared almost entirely purple or purple-blue; whereas the *Caryophyllus maximus dictus Hulo rubro-varius* had flowers of a deep red with striped, speckled and other variable patterns with white.

Some flowers had appeared (or perhaps been quietly assisted in their appearance) in specific localities and were named after them.

This early 17th-century illustration includes a long Latin description that formed the 'names' of each plant. Basilius Besler, *Hortus Eystettensis*, vol. III: *Decimusquartius ordo collectarum plantarum aestivalium.*

The Oxford carnation had a large flower of a 'sadder red colour' but with a fine white marbling, although this compared unfavourably to the better speckled and striped 'King's Carnation' or the 'Granado' with its purple and white stripes and divisions. The 'London White' came predictably from London where many of the nurseries were located, as did the 'Westminster Gilloflower', but the 'Poole Flower' was surely geographically lax in being discovered at 'Cogshot' Castle in the Isle of Wight, 45 miles across the sea from Poole. Colours were the source of many names although sometimes were a little haphazard, or perhaps overambitious. The 'Bristow Blew' (blue) was actually described by Parkinson as light purple, and often changed its colour to blush or purple; the 'Blew Gilloflower' was round and handsome and usually a deep purple colour, except when it tended to the tawny; while the 'White Dover' was grey or light blush, except when it was the 'Red Dover', although it at least redeemed itself name-wise by actually originating in Dover.

As variations were produced in petal form beyond those that were seen in the wild, so the terms 'ruffled' or 'ruffling' appeared alongside the descriptions 'jagged', 'dented' or 'feathered', most often in connection with the pink. The inconsistency of the flower at this early stage of selection and 'breeding' (of which more in the next chapter) caused obvious frustrations to those attempting to corral them into named species, as when Parkinson declares of *Caryophyllus maximus chrystallinus*:

> the Chrystall or Chrystalline (for they are both one, however some would make them differ) is a very delicate flower when well marked, but it is inconsistent in the markes, being sometimes more striped with white and crimson red, and sometimes less, or little or nothing at all, and changing also to be wholly red or wholly blush.[7]

Some descriptions of the florist's art were just plain confusing: the red and white striped cambersine (*Caryophyllus maximus cambersine dictus*) was described as being somewhat like the 'sauadge' (savage) carnation, but not as crimson, so perhaps more like the daintie, but then again not as 'comely' – although of course there was great variation in it. Some names seem to defy explanation. Did the 'Turkey Gilloflower' actually come all the way from Turkey, one wonders? The 'Brassill Gilloflower' is extremely unlikely to have come from Brazil at that period, although Parkinson's description of its 'sad purple' colour and 'meane size' make it seem an unlikely candidate for a respectable plant nursery. 'The Pageant', Parkinson tells us, was suitably 'pleasant to behold', although apparently distressingly common, which made it much less respected than a rarer plant. The 'Sad Pageant', however, would seem to be a contradiction in terms, although as the Italian *carne-vale* (carnival) is meant to derive from a 'farewell to meat' and one last celebratory feast before the famine of Lent, thereby sharing the same root of *carne* as the carnation, a 'Sad Pageant' carnation might be appropriate.

Perhaps the most evocative of the sixteenth-century names for carnations and pinks are those that refer back to the nurserymen or florists whose dedication and good fortune created them, and the families, friends and patrons they are thought to have honoured. 'Master Tuggie's Princess' is one, alongside 'Master Tuggie's Rose Gilloflower'. The nurseryman Ralph Tuggie specialized in some of the 'rarities' and florists' flowers that so delighted florists of the seventeenth century and his name spread far and wide. Tuggie's nursery was in Westminster and may have also been responsible for the 'Westminster Gilloflower' that was also known rather confusingly as the 'Lustie Gallant'. Thomas Johnson, in his 1633 revised edition of John Gerard's *Herball* (originally published in 1597), described Tuggie as having 'whilst he lived exceeded most, if not all of his time, in his care, industry and skill, in raising, increasing and preserving of these plants'.[8] Despite having nine children, all born between 1621 and 1632, Ralph's wife Catherine Tuggie took charge of the nursery after Ralph's death in 1632, and became renowned in turn for her gilleflowers, colchicums and auriculas. Thomas Johnson, having first praised Ralph Tuggie, claimed that Mrs Tuggie's 'nurserie . . . in the excellence and varietie of these delights exceedeth all that I have seen.' The nursery retained its good name and the name of its gilleflowers throughout the life of Catherine, who was able to pass the business to her son Richard on her death in 1651. One wonders whether it was Catherine or one of her daughters who was the original 'Master Tuggie's Princess', or was it the flower itself that Ralph adored? Whatever its origin, the 'Princess' was a rich and fair tawny with flowers as big as the 'Prince' or 'Chrystal', striped and marbled with veins and stripes and deeply jagged at the edges. The whole, as Parkinson declares, was 'exceedingly delightsome'. 'Tawny' gilloflowers appear to have been largely the stock of a John Wittie, who we can imagine was peeved to find his 'great tawny gilloflower' outshone by various of the Tuggie clan.

Master Bradshawe was another nurseryman who created new varieties listed by Parkinson. His 'Dainty Lady' was apparently very neat and small with a fine and small 'jagge' (the pinked edge of the petal) and a 'delightful' mix of red and white on the different part of the flower and its undersides. 'Davey's Rainbow' was later a favourite of the florist and nurseryman Thomas Hogg, again commemorating an individual florist or nurseryman. In France, namings appear to have taken a rather more classical turn, at least for the carnation lover Louis Boulanger, who named his *oeillets* after the Roman emperors Caesar and Pompey and the greatest ruler of them all, Alexander.[9] Problems arose not just in deciding what was a new variety or cultivar and what was a variation on those already known, but in maintaining them in their forms. 'Master Tuggie's Rose Gilloflower', for example, was said to be 'onely possessed by him that is the most industrious preserver of all natures beauties', having been raised from a seed of a more common tawny, with all the dangers inherent in that for back-sliding to its original form and colouring rather than maintaining the shape and colour of a 'red rose campion'.

Parkinson was one of the last great English herbal botanists and his admiration of the dianthus as a flower planted for pleasure, as well as physic, was taken up by the 'florists' or lovers of flowers (and especially rarities of new varieties) who dominated the floral world of the late seventeenth and eighteenth centuries. Thomas Hanmer (1612–1678) was such a man. His father, Sir John, 1st Baronet, was MP for Flintshire and had a strong tendency towards Puritanism rather than a love of fancy flowers, but in the years after succeeding him in 1624 Sir Thomas Hanmer turned to the Royalist side and during the Civil War raised troops to support Charles I, for whom he had been a cup-bearer. Perhaps Hanmer had learned his love of flowers at court, where both the king and more especially his queen, Henrietta Maria, led a court steeped in masques, imagery, gardens and allegories of heavenly summer come to earth in the shape of the Caroline court. Henrietta Maria was after all known as the 'Rose and Lily Queen' and engaged gardeners and designers from across Europe to create her royal gardens. During the interregnum, Hanmer retired to his Flintshire estate and garden at Bettisfield, where he contented himself with corresponding with men such as John Evelyn (himself a royalist) and the botanist John Rae, a friend and neighbour who described Hanmer's garden as incomparable and the man himself as one of the greatest authorities on garden plants and flowers.[10] Rae himself listed 91 varieties of carnation and pink.[11] He was so impressed with Hanmer's collection, which included both rare tulips and the new 'double carnations', that he dedicated his 1665 book, *Flora*, to him.[12] Hanmer did not publish a book of his own, but he did compile a 'Garden Book', dated 1653–9, which survived in manuscript form for the following 280 years, finally being published in 1933 by the garden historian Eleanour Sinclair Rohde.[13] Disconcertingly the list of names Hanmer gives us for the gilliflower or the French *oillet*, as he calls them, do not bear any recognizable relationship to those given to us by Parkinson. Instead, we get a distinctly European slant to the namings, perhaps resulting from Hanmer's having lived in France for some years. Among the scarlet gillyflowers he names the 'Nonpareille', the 'Pucelle', 'Incarnadine de Bland', 'French Merveille Piccolomini' (this is surely an Italian version come to Hanmer's Welsh garden via France!), 'Belle Astrea', 'Belle Eudique' and 'Belle Belin'. 'Cher Amy' perhaps hints at a French nurseryman's love in the same way as 'Master Tuggie's Princess'.

The nurserymen and florists of the Low Countries and Austria are also represented in Hanmer's list, if not by their own names, at least by names of those associated with the region: 'Admirall [*sic*] of Zealand', 'General Dortoon', 'General Coman', 'Alexander of Holland', 'Van Koell' and 'Hertoch Leopold'. Inspiration for the increasing wealth of names and titles came also from wider afield both geographically and historically: 'Prince of Wales', 'Queen Hesther' (crimson and white with a large flower), 'The King of Portugal', 'Venetian', 'Prince of Condé' and 'Grand Turban'. The appearance of these 'dedicatory' names, usually bestowed not by a royal or aristocratic gardener but by a nurseryman or florist trying to curry favour, was to set a pattern for the future as the carnation and even the humbler pink took on a welter of aristocratically named varieties in the eighteenth and nineteenth centuries. This tendency to aristocratic honorifics could result in some bizarre statements in nurserymen's catalogues. According to one writer, for example, 'Napoleon III' could be difficult to keep alive, being a weakling of the carnation world, which bears no resemblance to the real Napoleon III, president and emperor of France and an active man who lived to be 65 years of age. Back in the mid-seventeenth century one can only hope that the king of Portugal was suitably impressed with 'his' carnation – one of the newest varieties which boasted, according to Hanmer, 'a kind of deepe murrey and white',[14] being of reasonably large flower. After this jaunt around Europe in nomenclature it is almost a relief to discover the more traditional 'Bezar's Tawny' among those that found a home with Hanmer in Bettisfield.

Hanmer follows his list of names with a caution to carnation growers that even when kept in good earthenware pots over the winter,

there is no flower more subject to dye [die], either with the frosts of wynter, the wynds of spring, the violent drought

The 'Louis Napoleon' carnation, from the horticulture journal *Flore des serres et des jardins de l'Europe* (1845–80), handcoloured lithograph.

and heate of sommer, or much raines at any time of yeare, therefore they need an experienced and careful gardiner to looke to them and one must be stored with great numbers of them to have a sufficient quantity in Sommer, for many will dye every yeare, let the care of them bee never soe great.

Two whole pages of instructions follow for the tending and preservation of the plants with almost hourly tasks, including frequent shaking of earwigs from the sticks that the flower stalks should be tied to for support. In 1671, while the gardener and essayist John Evelyn was busy making his new garden at Deptford in London, Hanmer sent him many other plants, with accompanying instructions to plant as soon as possible and water well. He wrote to Evelyn that

> I thought once to have ventured some gilliflowers having two years since raised some very good ones from seed (which I never did before, nor I think shall never again, because the wet in England hinders the ripening of the seed more than in Holland and Flanders) but there is such store of excellent ones all about London, that I had not the confidence to adventure any to your view, and I doubted whether being so long on the way would not kill them.[15]

We know from a later book that Holland sent 'immense numbers' of carnation plants to England, selling them 'at mean rates to gardeners, who sell them again to others that delight in flowers, commonly at twelve pence a layer, but the truth is most of these mercenary fellows are deceitful'.[16]

Evelyn's garden at Deptford was to become his inspiration and his 'laboratory' as he collected plants from as many corners of the world as were then known and sheltered them in its walls, planting and ripening, dividing, setting and seeding, so that the gardens became famous for both their design and their planting. In his

Kalendarium Hortense or The Gard'ners Almanac, Evelyn is distressingly reticent about the names of the carnation varieties he has in the garden, lumping them all under 'carnations and pinks', but in his most ambitious work, *Elysium Britannicum*, never published in his lifetime, he makes frequent mention of carnations both in special pots ('carnation pots') and in the plant borders and lists the names that had become well known by the mid-seventeenth century plus later arrivals. His list, like Hanmer's, with which there is some degree of overlap, is again a mix of traditional and new. 'Passe me Not', 'Painted Lady', 'Common Haloe' and 'Fayre Maids of Kent' were all traditional English names, but the 'Bel Infanta', 'The Dukes Amarillus' and 'Prince Rupert' are later additions.[17] Evelyn himself evidently found the names confusing, stating of the scarlet and white varieties that 'Some of these and of all the other classes are known by severall other names which yearely beare according to the fancy of the raiser or possessor.' He ends his list of about 150 named varieties, sorted according to their colour, with the faintly despairing 'and hundreds more to be reduced into what order you please'.[18]

Nurserymen and botanists were not the only ones to publicize the names of the plants in their care, and it is to a poet that we owe our next list of intriguing names. Commissioned from Mathew Stevenson (fl. 1654–85) for the occasion of a late seventeenth-century competition or 'feast', 'At the Florists Feast in Norwich: Flora Wearing a Crown' lists names of the most popular fancy carnations of the day. The poet first disposes of the charms of the 'lily and the rose' (though he admits them as flowers of the king and queen), and the violet, cornflower and marigold are likewise scorned for the 'cabinet of treasures' at the August 'Carnation' feast. The poet then lists the most important carnations one by one:

> The *Painted Lady*, (think it though no taint
> Unto her beauty, for 'tis natures paint)
> The rare *Diana*, not shee whome we find
> In the wild woods, noe, this is garden kinde;

On whom a man may looke, and, smiles importune,
Without the danger of a horned fortune.
Next this sweet dame, There's the *Begrovenere*,
The lovely *Comans*, The peerlesse *Grampeere*,
Speckemakers white, Taunies cumbers cornation
Are flowers which nothing want but admyration.
The *murry, mullion*, and the *Baljudike*
T'were plenteous want of wisdome not to like;
The faire *Amelia*, the *Nymph Royall,* and
The *Turks cap*, the *Adonis*, the *Le grand*,
The *Hugonant, Appelles*, and *French marble*,
Are such whose praise, a phylomel should warble.
The *Oxford* had attended on the crowne,
But that to tell you truth he's out of towne.
Here's the gray *Hulo* though, and white *Cornation*,
Would challenge more then common commendation.[19]

Thomas Hogg the nurseryman, who launched into publication to promote his achievements in the floral world of carnations, pinks, auriculas, polyanthus, ranunculus, tulips, hyacinths, roses and other florists' flowers, listed as many as 154 varieties of carnation by the time of the 1822 edition of his work, and many more pinks and picotees. Hogg included many 'sports',[20] which he said had occurred in the summer of 1818, which had been very hot and dry and appeared to Hogg and his companion florists to have given rise to this phenomenon. These 'sports', also known as 'run flowers' in the eighteenth century, were a mystery to nurseries and florists and Hogg records that 'I frankly confess, I can neither comprehend nor explain, and the opinions I have ventured to offer . . . are founded altogether on hypothesis, conjecture and uncertainty.'[21] Some suggested that it was the action of the sun's heat on the flowers 'whilst in embryo' that caused the petals to change colour to that most predominant (usually red) colour, while others argued that it was 'owing to the fixed alkalis not being properly neutralized by the vegetable and vitriolic acids that caused the natural colours to be discharged'. Hogg quite reasonably admitted that he did not understand the last argument, being 'not chemist enough', and instead agreed with gardeners who felt that carnations had a greater risk of producing sports in rich soil, suggesting that in order to restrict the 'danger and risk' of sporting, the amount of compost in the loam mix should be restricted and the plant kept cooler.

The carnations that Hogg managed to prevent from 'running' off to pale imitations of themselves, or mutating to a range of other colours and markings, included a number whose names again reflected the heroes and events of the day and those active nurseries and florists who had created them, rather than those lost in the Tudor mists of time. History learned through flowers. Twenty-four years after the eponymous battle, Hogg boasted 'Tate's Waterloo', 'Wilson's Lord Nelson' and 'Mason's Duke of Wellington', and fresh from the battle-fields of the American Civil War was 'Phillip's Lord Harrington', accompanied by a sprinkling of aristocracy including 'Plummer's Lord Manner', 'Chaplain's Lord Duncan', 'Humphrey's Duke of Clarence' and 'James's Lord Craven' – literally English 'flowers of the realm'. 'Sharpe's Defiance', sounding like a later work of fiction by Bernard Cornwell, was suitably military and one can only hope the (unknown) colourings did not clash when sharing a flower bed with 'Hoyle's General Washington' or cause havoc with Weltje's 'Maid of Honour'.

While Hogg's carnations were of a largely nationalistic flavour (albeit with a nod to *amour* through 'Stone's Venus'), the yellow picotees had an altogether more Continental outlook. As Hogg admitted, the yellow picotee was even more difficult to grow in England and the Netherlands than the normally fretful carnation, needing a dry warm atmosphere, and so most of the varieties came over from Italy, France, Germany, Prussia and Switzerland with names to match.[22] 'Napoleon' brushed leaves with 'Louis Seize' and 'Le Dauphin de France', while the 'Prince of Orange' and 'Count de Grasse' might have shared a bed with either the 'Maid of Orleans'

The carnation Lady Ardilaun, named after the first wife of the wealthy philanthropist 1st Baron Ardilaun, who was famed for his gardens.

or the 'Maid of Magdeburg'. Perhaps most exotically named of the picotees was the 'Princess Esterhazy'. Originally (in real life) Princess Maria Theresia of Thurn and Taxis had been born in 1794 in Regensburg, Free Imperial City of the Holy Roman Empire, and was related through her mother, Duchess Therese of Mecklenburg-Strelitz, to the popular English Queen Charlotte, also originally of the royal house in Mecklenburg-Strelitz. As if these titles and origins were not enough, in 1833 Maria Theresia married Paul Anthony, 8th Prince Esterhazy of Galantha (becoming Her Serene Highness the Princess Esterhazy of Galantha, Princess of Thurn and Taxis), and through her husband's diplomatic career was admired and celebrated throughout Europe. A lot for a small picotee to live up to. Among all these famous personages and far-flung places, there was still the occasional oddity of Englishness. Included in the pinks Hogg listed in his 1822 catalogue were, for example, 'Beauty of Ugliness', 'Berkshire Buffalo' and 'Agripinna', and who would have found themselves drawn to the commonly named 'Farmer Pickering' or 'Hopkin's Scarecrow' when 'Lady Hamilton' or 'the 'Countess of Pembroke' were available? Among this welter of choices, Hogg listed some of his own production: a scarlet carnation known as 'Hogg's Sirius', a purple flake carnation called 'Hogg's Mrs Siddons' (named after the famous tragedienne Sarah Siddons, who died in 1831), and rose and pink flake carnations 'Hogg's Queen' and 'Hogg's Paddington Beauty' – some reward for all his hard work and struggles to understand the quixotic nature and complex naming of the carnation.

At the other end of the social scale to the 'Princess Esterhazy' is 'Mrs Sinkins', introduced to the floral world in 1868 and now one of the best-loved dianthus varieties. Mr Sinkins was the superintendent of Slough Workhouse in the mid-nineteenth century and an avid carnation grower. Among those growing in his garden was a pure white, heavily scented flower which caught the eye – and the nose – of Charles Turner, nurseryman. Turner bargained with Mr Sinkins for slips of the plant, and on the consideration that it was named after his wife, the romantic workhouse keeper allowed the plant to be launched onto the market, where it still remains. A little later it was joined by 'Miss Sinkins' in pink, but many still favour the older of the two.

If one were pushed to choose a favourite carnation name, however, I think mine would have to be the wonderful 'Seattle Shaggy'. This name was used by Washington plantswoman Léone Bell when she introduced the plant to her friends in the 1980s. After research

Dianthus 'Mrs Sinkins' in author's garden.

into the origins of the pale pink double flower, with its crimson eye and strong fragrance, Mrs Bell finally concluded that it was actually the 'Gloriosa', a fine carnation-pink hybrid first grown in Scotland during the late 1700s, and then imported to America, before being supposedly lost there. However, rather than reverting to its original name, she retained 'Seattle Shaggy', with its imagery of ruffled petals and its hints back to Elizabethan namings, although with a thoroughly modern origin.

three
Nature's Bastards:
From Divinity to Blasphemy

There are carnations in the garden
in colours of ruby red,
pure white and blossom pink
and some pink with deep purple inside
and others purple-blue.

I smell the sweet fresh flowers
and look at colours
hue as if by magic
into each other.

GERT STRYDOM, b. 1964, 'Carnations in the Garden'

On a cold February afternoon in 1720 a nervous Thomas Fairchild displayed to the Royal Society in London a plant at once unique and blasphemous. *Dianthus caryophyllus barbatus*, a hybrid between a sweet william and a carnation, had, according to the presentation made to the Royal Society, been accidentally produced in Fairchild's Hoxton nursery. That Fairchild (1667–1729), a trained nurseryman, should claim that a breakthrough in the understanding of plant reproduction took place 'by accident' appears at the least unusually self-effacing, if not oddly disingenuous, until one realizes the implications. To produce a new variety or cultivar had long been held to have a dubious standing, lurking between the province of a deity and of a florist. To create

These artfully coloured carnations, depicted on a postcard,
are the product of paint rather than nature.

an entirely new species, as was later claimed by Fairchild's friend Richard Bradley to actually have been the case, was one step too far – and smacked of playing God.

Fairchild was a practical nurseryman rather than a scientist and was not himself a member of the august Royal Society to which his achievement (accidental or otherwise) was presented by his friend Patrick Blair, a doctor and amateur botanist who had just published a book of botanical essays appropriately dealing with the contentious topic of plant reproduction. Hybridization, the production of new varieties or species by cross-breeding, was theoretically unknown to both nurserymen and scientists in the early eighteenth century. 'Improvements' or changes in flower colours, leaf size, hardiness and so on were created either by chance such as a 'sport', or by selectively and continuously physically removing or 'weeding out' those furthest from the ideal aimed at. In addition some florists and nurserymen attempted to create change by altering the environment in which

This nurseryman or florist is raising his plants in pots as recommended, 1867 etching by Mary Turner.

the plant grew. The very notion of plant 'breeding' with all its sexual overtones was strenuously denied until the late seventeenth century. The scientist and naturalist philosopher Francis Bacon declared in 1627 that 'generation by copulation certainly extendeth not to plants.' In 1674 even John Ray, one of the foremost botanists of the day, could not convincingly explain how seeds came to be fertilized, nor how variation could be achieved reliably or by anything other than the established methods. Anxious as he was to achieve distinction in his exploration of plant variations, Ray concluded with a suitably religious orthodoxy that one could not devise new categories or species of plants, because 'God having finished his works of creation, that is consummated the number of species, in six days'. It was not for us to attempt to add to God's ordained number.

However, by the late 1670s several more scientifically minded horticulturalists and botanists had started to hint that all was not as innocent as it had seemed in the flower borders, and within two decades of Ray's pronouncement experiments on the role of pollen and seed, and the identification of male and female parts on plants (sometimes on the same plant), had led at least to the theoretical possibility that humans might strike out into pastures new that God had neglected to create. In 1694 Rudolf Camerarius of the University of Tübingen in Germany insisted that plants 'behave to each other as male and female . . . not as an analogy or figure of speech, but actually and literally as such'. Camerarius went on to anticipate Fairchild's work by saying, 'the difficult question, which is also a new one, is whether a female plant can be fertilized by a male of another kind, the female hemp by the male hops . . . and whether, and in what degree altered, a seedling will arise therefrom.' By the time the Royal Society heard the explanation of Fairchild's 'accidental' hybridization they had been warned by men such as Nehemiah Grew (a doctor and botanist) and Marcello Malphigi (an Italian doctor) that plants did indeed appear to have seeds that were in some way fertilized, in common with animals or, as Grew phrased it, 'came at first out of the same Hand and were the contrivances of the same Wisdom'. What

Sex in the garden: a close-up image of a *Lavatera* reveals details of the sex life of plants, which was undreamt of by early florists.

had not changed was the belief that God had invented the system, whatever it was, and it was for him alone to attempt any changes. Patrick Blair, who rose to present Fairchild's mule to the Royal Society on that cold February evening in 1720 (as well as his own published work on plant reproduction), was to change all that.

First of all Blair reported on an experiment carried out by Thomas Knowlton, then a gardener at Offley Place, which 'proved' through different methods of wheat sowing that a union of male and female flowers was necessary to fructification. He then continued on to Fairchild's 'discovery' of a new garden plant 'of a middle nature between a Sweet William and a carnation' which had been found at a place in Fairchild's nursery where seeds of the two different flowers had been 'scattered accidentally' and mingled together. Fairchild opened the precious packet that had accompanied him to the meeting, and demonstrated the unique flower in its pressed and preserved state (it was after all February, a time of year when even a hybridized carnation might shirk from flowering). Blair then further revealed that Knowlton, the gardener who had sexualized wheat growing, had also 'found' a very similar crossing of species in the garden at Offley. With its astounding implication for science, horticulture and theology it seems incredible that the Royal Society did not close the evening with either celebrations or riots, or perhaps both. Instead they calmly proceeded through a talk on a meteor observed in Dublin the month before and a description of the birth of 'Siamese twins', before Fairchild himself treated them to a display of a chrysalis on its slow and patient way to becoming a moth, itself a phenomenon only identified in the late seventeenth century by the female naturalist Maria Sibylla Merian.

The delicate flower of Fairchild's 'mule' (the term 'hybrid' was not to come into common usage until some time after this) became a short-lived fashion, being reproduced by cuttings from the Hoxton original, as it was infertile as all hybrids are. With its delicate narrow leaves and stems from its carnation parent and the trumpet flowers of its other, it was officially recorded as 'Mule Pink Fairchild' or *Dianthus caryophyllus barbatus*. Erasmus Darwin made mention of it in his extended verse *The Botanic Garden* in 1791:

> Caryo's sweet smile, Dianthus proud admires
> And gazing burns with unallow'd desires;
> With sighs and sorrows her compassion moves,
> And wins the damsel to illicit loves.
> The monster-offspring heirs the father's pride,
> Mask'd in the damask beauties of the bride.

Long after the popularity of the 'monster-offspring' had waned, its legacy lived on both in modern hybridization and also in the annual church sermon which the anxious Fairchild left a bequest for in his will. Perhaps still unsure whether he had overstepped the mark and trespassed into the territory of the deity, Fairchild bequeathed £25 (to be placed out at interest for the payment of twenty shillings a year) to provide for a sermon on the topic of 'The Wonderful World of God in the Creation or on the Certainty of the Resurrection of the Dead proved by the Certain Change of the Animal and Vegetable Parts of the Creation'. Known for many years as the 'Vegetable Sermon', Fairchild's bequest was fulfilled for many years at St Leonard's Church on Hackney Road in London before transferring to St Giles Cripplegate in 1981, where it still continues. Thomas Fairchild's own gravestone, meanwhile, has been rescued from the neglect of time and now boasts a new garden around it, while posies of pinks frequently decorate the headstone of the man who vied with God to create a new carnation and turned the divine and incarnate flower to the purpose of science.

Sinfulness in the shape of bastardy had already been achieved by florists seeking to improve the carnation's divine colouring several decades before Fairchild had created his blasphemous 'mule'. Unaware of the sex life of plants, florists had given rise to these 'bastards' by a process of hopeful selection combined with accidental mutations – a process that had also overseen the 'Tulipmania' of the early seventeenth century in the Netherlands and parts of northern Europe. As early as 1597, John Gerard, in his *Herball, or General Historie of Plants*, stated with some apprehension that

Gravestone of Thomas Fairchild, decorated by the author of a blog on Spitalfields.

There are at this day under the names of Caryophllus . . . comprehended divers and sundrie sorts of plants, of such variable colours, and also severall shapes, that a great and large volume would not suffice to write of every one at large in particular; considering how infinite they are, and how every yeere, every climate and every countrie bringeth foorth new sortes, such as have not been heretofore written of; . . . Likewise there be sundrie sorts of Pinks comprehended under the same title, which shall be described in a severall chapter.

In fact Gerard managed to marshal this seemingly uncontrollable outbreak of what would later be known as species and varieties into a mere six pages, with an extra two pages for sweet johns and sweet williams. In the text and illustrations he gave pride of place and leading role to the 'Great Carnation Gilloflower and the Clove Gilloflower', which he records as only differing from each other in appearance in the size of the leaves and the flowers rather than the form. The great carnation gillyflower did not survive wet or cold weather as well as the clove gillyflower and should, according to Gerard, always be kept in pots, whereas the clove gilloflower might be planted in the ground. Hugh Platt in his *Floraes paradise* of 1608 talks longingly of carnations raised by the warmth of a stove by Master Jacob 'of the Glass-House'. Rather than a floral glasshouse, this was actually a warm spot in a workshop dedicated to the making of glass objects, and Master Jacob was Jacob Verzellini, a native of the 'glass-makers' island' of Murano. Jacob had travelled to Antwerp before coming to London, and although his glass-making techniques came from Italy one suspects his carnations hailed from the Netherlands.

These, then, were the foremost garden carnations of the early seventeenth century, and would tempt the gardener and nurserymen to play God. In Shakespeare's *The Winter's Tale* (c. 1610) the innocent Perdita, brought up by a shepherd in the simple ways of the rustics, refers to 'carnations and streak'd gillyvors', which she says 'some call nature's bastards'. Despite the royal and worldly Polixenes' protestations on their behalf, Perdita refuses to countenance the thought of slips of these floral transgressors of nature in her 'rustic garden' and in a scene which also refers to Perdita's original regal parentage (then unknown to either of the characters), Polixenes argues:

> Yet nature is made better by no mean
> But nature makes that mean: so, over that art
> Which you say adds to nature, is an art
> That nature makes. You see, sweet maid, we marry
> A gentler scion to the wildest stock,
> And make conceive a bark of baser kind
> By bud of nobler race: this is an art
> Which does mend nature, change it rather, but
> The art itself is nature. (IV, 4)

Shakespeare thus not only places the 'streak'd gillyvor' at the heart of the play and its discussion on the role of nature versus nurture, but integrates into this contemporary discussion on the part man plays in the universe by the marrying of one plant to another to create new stock. By the time the play was first published in the First Folio in 1623, Perdita would have had several 'streak'd gillyvors' to choose from had she relented and agreed more wholeheartedly with Polixenes' arguments, rather than ending the discussion with the brief and seemingly grudging statement: 'So it is.' Between the publication of *The Winter's Tale* and the presentation of Fairchild's mule at the Royal Society lay a period of almost a hundred years, during which time florists and nurserymen would strive to create myriad 'Nature's bastards', although none so challenging as that simple act of introducing a carnation to a sweet william.

In the late sixteenth century the sudden appearance of the striped Rosa Mundi as a natural 'sport' of the *Rosa gallica officionalis* had caused a sensation. The rose became a treasured prize among collectors such as Sir Thomas Hanmer, who described the flower in his unpublished 'Garden Book' of 1659. The combining of colours in piebalds or streaks, as contemporary descriptions called them, became a fascination of all plant collectors, whether their fancy be roses, tulips or carnations. For John Gerard, the only colours that the confusing range of carnations and pinks were likely to be discovered in were whites, reds, 'purples' and pinks, with leaves 'jagged' or feathered and occasionally 'doubled'. Only the sweet john was available in a 'confused' speckled form and only then in 'some of our London gardens'. Only one garden (Gerard's own) boasted a yellow gillyflower. But all that was soon to change. In contrast to the mere six pages devoted to the carnation, pink and sweet william by Gerard, in 1629 John Parkinson devoted fourteen pages to the various forms of dianthus, and by 1704, when he published his final volume on the *History of Plants*, the botanist John Ray would be able to list over 360. However, what they all had in common was the ability to mutate and change, most especially when grown from seed. As Parkinson noted in his *Paradisi in sole, paradisus terrestris* of the yellow or orange tawny gillyflower:

> this kind is more apt to beare seeds than any other . . . and being sowen yeelde wonderfull varieties both of single and double flowers: some being of lighter or deeper colour than the mother plants: some with stripes in most of the leaves: Others are striped or spotted, like a speckled carnation of gilloflower in divers sorts both single or double: some again are wholly of the same colour, like the mother plant, and are either more or less double than it, or else are single with one row of leaves, like unto a Pink, and some of these likewise eyther wholly of a crimson red deeper or lighter, or variably spotted, double or single as a Pink, or blush eyther single or double, and but very seldom white: yet all of them in their greene leaves little or nothing varying or differing.

Striped flowers on this work bag from 1717 show the fashionable carnations of the period.

In other words, the leaves may look the same but what the flowers will look like is anybody's guess!

This mutability, little understood in an age before the sexual life of plants was dreamt of, had resulted in two contradictory conclusions among the ever-burgeoning number of flower fanciers and florists of the seventeenth and early eighteenth centuries: if one wanted a specific form of carnation or pink it must surely be just a matter of time before it came along in the profligacy of shapes, sizes and patterns with which God had blessed the divine flower; but following on, if one wanted to produce or replicate a specific form of flower, then allowing the plants to randomly sow seed was not going to help. Instead there would have to be human intervention.

During the years of 'Tulipmania' in northern Europe, several methods had been used to try to influence the colour or shape of flowers – a particular challenge as tulips take several years to come to flower from the seed stage and growing and dividing bulbs was slow and unreliable. Adding coloured dyes or other materials to the soil in the hope that it would influence the final colour was a popular (if unsuccessful) method. Blood or brick dust poured onto the soil close to a white tulip, for example, might be expected to result in a white and red tulip. Coal dust might nudge a red bulb towards purple and even the much sought-after black or midnight blue. Halving a bulb of a red tulip and one of white and then tying the two halves together and burying them was also a popular experiment and, given that the desired 'flaming' of red or crimson and white was actually caused by a virus to which the truncated and weakened bulbs were more susceptible, may even have meant that on occasions the process achieved the desired end. Sir Hugh Platt offered his readers advice on making 'single flowers doubled' by the phases of the moon which would surely have troubled the more puritanically minded, as the moon and its phases were the Devil's work. According to Platt's *Floraes paradise*, gillyflowers, pinks, roses, daisies and tulips could double if one

Remove a plant of stock gilliflowers when it is a little wooded and not too green, and water it presently; do this three days after the full Moon and remove it twice more before the change. Do this in barren ground, and likewise three days after the new full Moon, remove again; and then remove once more before the change. Then at the third full Moon

. . . remove again, and set it in very rich ground, and this will make it to bring forth a double flower.

Adding coal or blood to the soil does not influence the eventual colour of a flower whether it be tulip or dianthus (although perversely, once grown and flowered, a picked carnation flower can be transformed by being placed in coloured water); and continually uprooting and replanting a seedling, regardless of the whereabouts of the moon, is unlikely to lead to a healthy and happy flower. Eventually carnation fanciers were left with the slow and painstaking methods of selection either through seed or slips.

John Evelyn in his 1666 *Kalendarium hortense* refers to sowing seeds of 'pinks, Sweet Williams, and Carnations' in March, but as we have seen, the seeds of the garden dianthus were regarded as particularly unreliable by the herbalists of the period. However, taking 'slips' or offshoots of plants and rooting them was a well-known practice in the medieval and Tudor world and was generally regarded as more reliable in its outcome. In *The Country Housewife's Garden* (1618), William Lawson recommended that in order to increase her stock of gillyflowers the housewife should 'take the slips (without shanks) three or four years and set anytime except in extreme frost'. It was only the smallest of steps from this random multiplication of stock to a florist taking slips only from the plants with a particular colour or shape or marking and hoping to gradually develop those characteristics. The first of the desired characteristics, as with the rose and the tulip, was the introduction of stripes or streaks, preferably of white on a darker red or purple background. These were becoming established enough to have a range of more or less distinct types and names by the time Parkinson wrote his *Paradisi in sole, paradisus terrestris* in 1629 (see Chapter Two) but despite the piebald pink being a more modest affair than the stripy rose or the flaming tulip, they were still regarded with suspicion outside the small clique of flower fanciers.

Across the channel there was similar confusion as to how to achieve the desired carnation colours. In the reign of Louis XIV, the gardener Louis Boulanger wrote an entire work on garden pinks and carnations, the *Jardinage des oeillets* (1647), that listed several different methods employed by florists, including pulverizing coarse soil and then taking the plant to

cut it in the sun and watered it little after the space of fifteen or twenty days with red water or yellow, or another tint then . . . they sow the seed of this flower of a colour contrary to the artificial water.

Others mixed seeds of the carnations with the roots of the wild blue-flowered chicory in the hope of producing a blue carnation 'as beautiful as it is rare', or combined carnation seeds with seeds of variegated flowers in the hope of striping their carnations. Boulanger's work was dedicated to Geoffrey Lullier, the 'Chevalier Seigneur of Orgeval & of Mal-Maison', a man who, despite being magistrate to royalty, councillor of the state and privy, and having other high-ranking duties, had apparently dedicated his leisure time to the cultivation of carnations in the 'terrestrial paradise of [his] agreeable abode in Paris'. Boulanger was one of the many *curieux fleuristes* in France in the mid-seventeenth century, who, like the florists of England, were anxious to assure society that their interests did not extend to the blasphemous. Indeed the anonymous author of *La Culture des fleurs* wrote that the necessity of tending one's flower parterre not only could, but should, be a reminder to tend to one's soul. In a passage reminiscent of Othello, who pronounced that 'Our bodies are our gardens, to the which our wills are gardeners', the author of *La Culture des fleurs* explained, 'You know well (my dear reader) that your parterre is a figure of your soul, and that one day it will serve in your condemnation in the judgment of God, if you neglected to cultivate the Plant of your Garden.' These florists therefore saw the veneration of flowers as a means of venerating God as well as the god of fashion. Cultivation of flowers became an exercise in the cultivation of the soul. Neither Boulanger, Lullier, his

Carnations and pinks were so popular in 18th-century France that the street-sellers were included in a book on *Les Cris de Paris* (Street Cries of Paris, 1738).

fellow *curieux fleuristes*, nor the anonymous author of *La Culture des fleurs* realized that the seed of the carnation was already carrying the pattern of a future plant within it and could not, however fervently one mixed it with seeds and stems of blue-flowered plants, change colour. That realization lay in the future, when the role of pistils, stamens and pollen and the very sexuality of plants was laid bare, and the divine became just that bit more sinful.

Almost two hundred years after Fairchild exhibited his 'accidental' hybrid at the Royal Society, the Royal Horticultural Society organized its first ever conference on hybridization. It was at the very close of the nineteenth century, a century famed for industrialization, innovation and empire, but as the chairman of the conference opined, hybridization had not kept pace with these changes. Hindered by doubts over both the science involved and the morality of the under-taking, few had been brave enough to follow in Fairchild's footsteps. Indeed the religious scruples of many members of the Royal Society, recorded in the conference minutes, dictated that hybrids were largely absent from Royal Horticultural Society shows unless they appeared to have 'ocurr[ed] naturally' or had been brought in from that den of iniquity, 'abroad'. In late Victorian society the bastard offspring of the divine flower still had the power to shock.

four
Florists, Weavers and Cottagers
ᘒᕽ

I hesitate not a moment to prefer the plant of a fine carnation
to a gold watch set with diamonds.
WILLIAM COBBETT (1763–1835), writer on rural and
agricultural issues of the eighteenth century

In seventeenth-century England the carnation led a double
life: a humbler, plainer version would delight in the small rural
plot, busy providing tonics for the downhearted, scented petals
for tisanes and posies, and fodder for bees; while rarer striped and
spotted versions would flaunt their stuff with 'trips out' to feasts,
pageants and competitive social gatherings where they inspired men
and women whose lives were woven with colour and pattern at work
and play. Born out of the tradition of craftsmen's guilds, florists'
societies began in England as early as the 1630s and expanded with
the influx of flower-loving Huguenot refugees from France through
the seventeenth century. Members of the societies were not botanists pondering deeply on the relationship between one plant and
another, or even professional nurserymen. Indeed Carl Linnaeus,
who created the sexually based system of binomial classification,
warned his fellow scientists that 'no sound botanist should ever
enter the [florists] societies.' Instead, the societies were filled by
those who rejoiced in the flower itself and its wonderful and unexpected variety, which might provide them with (literally) a winning
streak in what was a competitive social club.

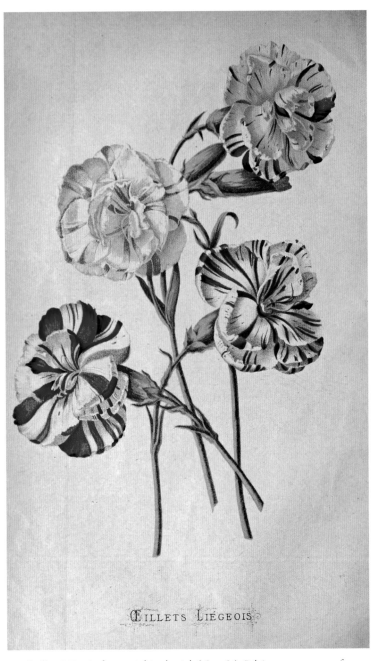

ŒILLETS LIÉGEOIS

Les Oeillets Liégeois, from *La Belgique horticole* (1851–85). Belgium was a source of many new varieties and combinations of *Dianthus* in the 18th and 19th centuries.

Described as 'Oeillet des fleuristes', in Edouard Maubert, *Dictionnaire universel d'histoire naturelle* (1841–9), this image captures a range of colours and types.

The first florists' societies concentrated on a small range of flowers – the carnation, tulip and ranunculus – soon joined by the auricula, hyacinth and polyanthus (known collectively as the 'shed' flowers from their need for protection by some form of shelter or 'shed'). Pinks only joined the hallowed selection in around 1770–90. By this time semi-double had been developed with less fringing of the petals, and these were favoured by the florists. By the late nineteenth century, the show flowers had expanded to include anemone, chrysanthemum, dahlia, hollyhock and pansy, as well as the much-debated picotee, and shows had become open to lovers of all manner of floral delights drawn from the spectrum of society. But all that was in the future. The seventeenth-century florists' societies drew their members from those who had money to finance their hobby and gardens to grow plants, often under canvas rather than expensive glass. As Samuel Gilbert made plain in his *Florists vade mecum* of 1682, 'the trifles adored amongst countrywomen' were 'of no esteem to a Florist who is taken up with things of more value'. By 1754 the growing of carnations outside with no protection at all was frowned on in many circles: in the *Scot's Gardener's Director* of that year, James Justice declared, 'It makes a better show to blow them in Pots upon a proper Stage, than to blow them in a slovenish manner in the open ground' ('blowing' having the meaning of 'flowering' in this period). Staging meant shelving, and this manner of display was most often used for the auricula, which could be grown in black-painted shelves in purpose-built 'theatres', although carnations and pinks could also benefit from such a theatrical display.

'Florist's feasts' were an essential adjunct to these early societies whose meetings were often held in public houses and might even include rules on how many drinks had to be purchased. Flowers would be submitted for judging at midday, followed at 1 pm by the dinner (an 'ordinary' or 'good ordinary'), and then judging at 4 pm, allowing for substantial drinking in the intervening hours. Reports in newspapers suggest that the final awards often took on a celebratory air, with one carnation show in Hackney (to find the best six 'whole blooming' carnations) being followed by 'a Grand Procession through the principal streets of Hackney, the Stewards being adorned with Crowns of Flowers, decorated in a beautiful manner with a Band of Musick attending them'.[1] The scene is positively Bacchanalian, and it is difficult to believe that, in the words of the article, the whole was conducted with the 'utmost Decency and Decorum'. The 'whole blooming' carnation of this particular show refers incidentally to the division at that time between those carnations whose large flowers usually resulted in them bursting the protective calyx, and those whose calyx remained intact. In 1631 the Norwich Florist

Society commissioned a play entitled *Rhodon and Iris* to be performed on the occasion of their spring meeting. Meetings in the following years were also marked by celebratory poems and theatrical displays. The society appears to have drawn members from the more cultured classes, including 'Gentleman of birth and quality in whose presence and commerce your cities welfare partly consists', at least according to the preface to the play. One member of the society was William Strode, chaplain to the bishop of Norwich, and author of a book of poems. The presence of Strode may have helped allay the fears of the Norwich Puritans of the period who were dubious about such feasts and frolics, accusing the florists of worshipping the goddess Flora, rather than the flowers of a Christian god, although a chaplain with a penchant for poesy and pinks was not something puritanical minds would have rejoiced in. The choice of the *Dios anthos* for one of the shows may also have caused disquiet among the more classically minded.

From an early association with 'gentry', the florists' societies settled down through the early eighteenth century to a membership mainly drawn from the middling classes, with showings from tradesmen, shop owners and clergymen. The latter category were well represented among plantsmen throughout the ages, often seeming to have had time on their hands and an ambivalent attitude towards transgressing the roles of God and man. It was one such clergyman, William Hanbury, who wrote *The Whole Body of Planting and Gardening* in 1771, which documented a shift among the membership of florists' societies towards the working man and 'manufacturer', or more correctly manufacturing hand. Reverend Hanbury was rector of Church Langton, Leicestershire, an area well known for its florists' societies, with two shows a year being given by most of these. In 1759 the July show of the Leicester Society of Florists included carnation categories for 'Whole Blowers', 'Picotees' and for a rather general 'best and fairest carnation'. By the 1790s, when only the summer show appears to have survived, up to sixteen different prizes were given for carnations and pinks, including those for 'broken', 'bizarre', 'flake' and 'piccatte [*sic*]', as well as the best seedling and several for different colour forms. Carnation shows also took place in nearby Mansfield and Atherstone, with even ladies invited to attend the latter.

In *Jackson's Oxford Journal* of 15 July 1772, no fewer than three florists' feasts were advertised in the county of Oxfordshire. On Monday 3 August at the Queen's Head in Banbury a large silver spoon was won by the shower of 'six best and completest whole blown carnations of different sorts', with the second-place entry earning five shillings and the best seedling carnation two shillings and six-pence. The following day the same categories were competed for at the Ship Inn in Oxford, where a large silver spoon was again on offer, and the next Monday, 10 August, the whole thing was replayed at the Swan Inn, Bicester. A silver spoon or ladle was a common prize, and a successful carnation or auricula grower might set their family up with an entire canteen of silver cutlery and accompanying silver snuffboxes. In Nottingham, florists' meetings appear to have started in 1775, with a carnation show at the Bull's Head public house where the usual carousings took place. In subsequent years, Nottingham show categories included carnations such as bizarres, flakes and picotees, the latter spelt myriad ways by the otherwise literate florists, including 'pickatee', 'piccatee' and 'piquette'.

The florist and nurseryman Thomas Hogg gave a rather jaundiced insight into the behaviour of some of his fellow florists in his *A Practical Treatise on the Culture of the Carnation, Pink, Auricula, Polyanthus, Ranunculus, Tulip, Hyacinth, Rose and Other Flowers* (1822) on the growth and culture of various florists' flowers, including the carnation. His salutary tale introduces a novice florist called Samuel Greenhorn who has secretly nurtured new varieties of carnations with which he hopes to sweep the prizes from the more experienced hands. Samuel travels 50 miles to London town to present his new seedling carnations to a florists' society show 'somewhere between Battersea and Chelsea' and is delighted when members of the society pour praise on his plants as he pours drink in their glasses. Proudly naming his new seedlings 'Greenhorn's Emperor', 'Greenhorn's Queen' and

'Lovely Margaret' (the latter after his wife), the naive Samuel pays for the drinks his new 'friends' have consumed well into the evening. Eventually left penniless by their voracious thirsts, he tries to escape, leaving his new seedlings behind him. Realizing that his pockets are finally empty the florists follow him out to the street, shouting abuse on the carnations they had so recently praised: his Emperor is a mere button, his Queen a buttercup and his lovely Meg a dirty red garter. In Hogg's words, 'Further, I dare not report.'

Although the fictitious Samuel Greenhorn may have learnt his lesson, many other working-class florists were ready to take his place at florists' shows and societies, trekking to their nearest towns in the hope of praise and perhaps prizes. In 1844 William Howitt, social commentator and poet, wrote of the many Derbyshire cottagers that 'are most zealous and successful florists', raising the finest carnations, ranunculus and polyanthus. Many of those plants bore the names of the villagers themselves, or the villages they came from. As Howitt observed, Hufton, Barker and Redgate are all people 'well known to me, who scarce were ever out of their own rustic districts, but whose names are thus made familiar all the country over'.[2] Hufton was a Derbyshire stocking maker who specialized in carnations and his fame was such that he was interviewed by the reporter for the *Midland Florist* in 1851. In the resulting article Hufton described his garden as 'facing south and sheltered from the north-east by extensive woods' – he utilized the woods to collect decaying leaves and 'willowdust', an almost magical 'dust' much prized by florists, and he found this, as the name suggests, in the gaps between willow branches. Unlike the fictional novice Samuel Greenhorn, Hufton was an accomplished shower of his carnations, often walking into Nottingham with a dozen pots in wooden boxes hanging from a yoke, like a milkmaid with pails. Hufton named one of his varieties after his landlord – another reminder that this was not a class of house owners but hard-working tenants – but the carnation for which he became best known was 'Hufton's Magnificent', a flake with white ground and red markings, which became one of the most prized varieties of the

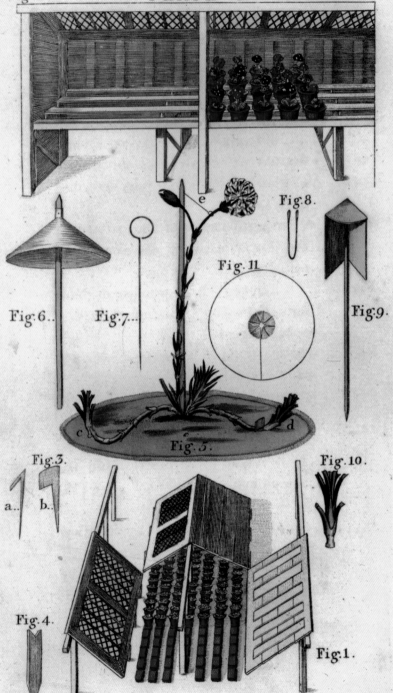

PLATE 8.

Fig. 2.

e

Fig. 8.

Fig. 11.

Fig. 6.

Fig. 7.

Fig. 9.

c   d

Fig. 5.

Fig. 3.

Fig. 10.

a..   b..

Fig. 4.

Fig. 1.

nineteenth century. Hufton's trade as a stocking maker, working from home, meant he could give his plants constant attention and was not hampered by either absence or a conflict between busy harvest periods for the farm labourer and the main period of carnation showing in later summer.

The Revd William Hanbury was the first to record an association between the carnation and the cloth weavers of the Midlands. In his late eighteenth-century book on planting and gardening for showing he recorded the growth in numbers of florists and florist's feasts among the working and middle classes and warned: 'Let not the Gardener be dejected if a weaver runs away with the prize as is often done.' Weavers worked long hours at their handlooms at home, often with the whole family involved in the trade and, as Hanbury recorded, they were available to rush out into the garden should any small shower or cold wind arrive to 'take the elegance off a prize auricula or carnation'. In fact according to Hanbury they were permanently poised to 'put [their] pots into the sun or again into the shade, can refresh them with air, or cover them at the least appearance of a black cloud'. He concluded that this state of constant alert enabled them to 'go at their work with more alacrity', although one wonders if time spent rushing in and out may not have resulted in a few flaws in the cloth or a diminution on their 'piece work' payments.[3] Although auriculas were favoured in the moist climate of the northern regions of Lancashire and Yorkshire by the home manufactories and weavers, the small hardy pink was taken up with enthusiasm by the miners of Durham and Northumberland and most especially the Paisley weavers of Scotland.

Initially not a florist flower, the pink had arrived on the exhibition stand with the creation in 1770 of the 'Duchess of Lancaster' – a laced pink with rounded, rather than serrated, petals and such exquisite markings that it was sold for the magnificent sum of £80. Double varieties soon appeared, including 'Lady Stoverdale', bred by the

'A View of the Winter Repository for Auriculas and Carnations', in James Maddock, *The Florists Directory* (1810).

nurseryman gardener James Major in about 1770. 'Lady Stoverdale', descended from the 'Duchess of Lancaster', had a dramatic band of black around the outer edge and a black centre on a background of pure white. Black and white seems an odd combination to be prized by men such as the Paisley weavers who worked in a swirl of colours, and there were other varieties to choose from with purples, crimsons and reds, although always on a white background. The Paisley Florist Society also provided pinks of their own – varieties such as 'Findlayson's Bonnie Lass' and 'Robertson's Gentle Shepherd', the latter also the name of a poem by the famous Paisley weaver Robert Tannahill, bringing together poetry and florists once again. The full acceptance of the pink into the close band of 'florists' flowers' was confirmed in 1792 when they appeared in an edition of James Maddock's *The Florist's Directory*, a copy of which was purchased by the Paisley Florist Society for use by all the members and loaned out to them 'as they stand in point of seniority',[4] although after being mislaid for some time is was ruled that it should be always brought back by its current holder and made available for quick reference at meetings. One can imagine the weavers poring over its illustrations of laced and patterned pinks, committing them to memory until the next meeting. The Reverend W. Ferrier, the dissenter minister for Paisley, suggested that the men use their floral interests not only in their leisure hours but to add interest to the patterns of their fabrics. The term 'Paisley' to describe the typical teardrop-shaped pattern comes from the town of Paisley, but the pattern itself originated in Kashmir, starting as a more rounded pine-cone shape not unlike the fan shape of Islamic and Persian depictions of carnations, before taking on the drooping attenuated style.

In the 1760s the weavers of Paisley numbered 4,400, but demand for their cloth grew so rapidly that by 1781 there were 6,800 hand-looms, of which 2,000 were weaving linen and 4,800 silk. By 1800 there were 23,900 home weavers and after Queen Victoria wore a Paisley shawl created by the weavers, the fashion redoubled. The first Florist Society was founded there in 1782 with the motto 'There is wondrous pleasure and delight in the cultivation of flowers', and the award of spades, rakes, trowels and forks as prizes in the annual shows reflected this need for the outdoor world. However, there was also a special competition, focusing each year on a different 'florists' flower'. In 1813 the society member who raised the best twelve pinks was awarded a snuff mill in the form of a ram's horn mounted in silver, an award that changed hands each year and is still lodged in the Paisley Museum. The statue of Flora that also graced the meetings has been lost over time, losing first her head in the nineteenth century, and then, when a replacement could not be found, her position: perhaps a puritan judgement on those who worshipped Flora as well as flowers?

The Paisley weavers were still cultivating pinks and carnations in the mid-nineteenth century when the garden writer John Claudius Loudon recorded that 'they are particularly remarkable in their taste

A shawl woven by Paisley weavers in the mid-19th century, with unusual combined patterns for paisley and flower.

This 1825 image of the town of Paisley, in Renfrewshire, depicts the open spaces on the fringes, but also the smoke that was eventually to eclipse the beloved Paisley pinks.

for objects which please the eye by their beauty, for such occupations for amusement that require nice [detailed] attention, and for various intellectual gratifications'. 'Their condition of improvement was', said Loudon, 'very rarely, if at all, to be paralleled among persons of the same rank of life',[5] with the possible exception of the literary miners of Leadhills, near Lanarkshire, who divided their leisure hours between horticulture and literature. The Paisley weavers were eventually to be credited with cultivating and naming 3,000 varieties of laced pink and were so influential in its development that the laced pink eventually became known as the 'Scotch Pink', and non-laced pinks were hardly thought worthy of showing. John Mcree, a Paisley muslin worker, was so proud of his pink, 'Paisley Gem', that he presented a plant to George III (1738–1820). 'Paisley Gem' is still with us, but most of the other carefully bred Paisley varieties were lost in the poor-quality air of the Industrial Revolution, as mills replaced the home loom. Many of the Paisley cloth patterns included carnations and pinks along the edges or within the paisley teardrop itself, with colours going far beyond those that could be achieved in real life.

Pinks and carnations had been popular subjects for embroidery for centuries prior to their celebration by the Paisley weavers, making their appearance on Tudor bed hangings, samplers and even eighteenth-century court dress. Elizabeth Talbot, Countess of Shrewsbury (*c.* 1527–1608), best known as Bess of Hardwick, included pinks in her series of embroidered flowers created to decorate the lavish Elizabethan Hardwick Hall, while the Elizabethan fashion for 'black work' embroidery resulted in pinks in black. In needlework the word for a design representing a cutting or specimen of a plant is 'slip', the very same word used for the cutting of a plant for grafting or growing on, the latter of which is common procedure in all types of dianthus. Most usually of canvas work (petit point), these slips were often sewn onto a ground fabric such as velvet or damask. Herbals such as John Gerard's of 1597 were often trawled for illustrations to base these slips on, so that the illustration of the real slip was in turn used to create the embroidered piece of the same name. The seventeenth-century botanical artist and

This modern paisley pattern combines tradition with light colouring and a more 'realistic' carnation flower.

Latiné   CARYOPHILLI.
Gallicé   OEILLETS.
Anglicé   IELIFLOWERS.

Carnation in a pattern book for embroidery and painting. 1586.

entomologist Maria Sibylla Merian created illustrations for her *Neues Blumenbuch* (New Flower Book) so that they could be used by fellow artists and needleworkers as well as those interested in plants. In France the Royal Gardener to Louis XIII, Pierre Vallet, was also the Royal Embroiderer and his book *Le Jardin du roy très chrestien, Loys XIII, roy de France et de Navare*, printed in Paris in 1623, was actually a pattern book for painters, embroiderers and tapestry weavers. His illustrations included the carnations 'Caryophillata flore purpureo' and the 'Caryophillata flore candida'. The illustrations are black-lined but a description of the colours in the accompanying listing ensured that embroiderers did not get carried away with impossible colours.

Vallet tells his readers that the specimen of 'C. flore purpureo' is 'De grosse laque avec du blanc & finie avec ladite laque' (Large glossy [or enamelled] with some white and finished with the said gloss), while the 'C. flore Candido' is 'De carmin tour à plat & finie avec le melme' (Of carmine tone flat and finished with the same).

Although most embroidery was based on individual plants, occasionally tapestries depicted entire gardens or landscapes, both real and imaginary. One such set are the famous Stoke Edith tapestries of the late seventeenth or early eighteenth centuries, a series of five showing various parts of the gardens. Possibly reflecting the gardens at Stoke Edith or, more likely, a fashionable 'composite' of garden features, the tapestries depict formal gardens replete with fountains, basins, statues, an orangery, alcoves and citrus trees in pots. Along the formal borders (or *bandes*) of the grass plats in each of the hangings are rows of carnations defined by their grey leaves and colourful heads. The tapestries depict all the flowers in perfect bloom, as are the tulips in the neighbouring *plates bandes*, and the citrus trees and wall fruits with their blooming borders below. This despite the presence in the 'Alcove Garden' tapestry of a dog, monkey and parrot who would wreak havoc in such a garden even if the seasons allowed such a mix of blooms.

Laced pinks, much beloved by the Paisley weavers, have an even closer etymological relation to needlework, as the term refers to that class of pinks that have intricate patterns of colouring on the petals – imitating an embroidered piece. At their greatest perfection the lacing is divided into three sections and named dark-laced or red-laced according to the depth of contrasting colour. While the weavers were cosseting the real thing, the 'grotto goddess' and mistress of botanic paper collage Mary Delany (1700–1788) was hard at work embroidering lace-edged pinks onto her fabulous court dress or mantua. The black silk dress, comprising a fabulously wide-hooped skirt, an over-gown and a stomacher, gave plenty of scope for the embroiderer's skill. Such dresses were frequently decorated with flowers and plants, and on occasion even entire garden scenes. In the case of Mrs Delany the ensemble was decorated with two hundred of her favourite flowers embroidered along the hems, while lily of the valley and pinks ran down the main stomacher. The pinks depicted by Mrs Delany were of the serrated kind and would not have met with the approval of florists' societies, who might however have accepted the auricula, pansies and roses that accompanied them.

The pinks that graced Mary Delany's dress moved in the highest circles of society, but the dianthus was also beloved of gardeners and embroiderers of the lower classes. Stitched samplers (from the French *essamplier*, something to be copied) first appeared in Europe in the sixteenth century, with a range of stitches and pattern which would later be used as a reference piece by the needlewoman or housewife. As the fashion grew they included patterns taken from embroidery and garden books of the period, and the fanlike carnation

One of the thousand paper collages created by Mary Delany in the late 18th century.

with its simplistic petals was often included in the floral motifs. In 1696 Elizabeth Mackett included carnations or pinks, seen not in profile but as though flattened in a flower press, with their typical edges and centres of colour. By the eighteenth century English samplers often included rows of plants, or small areas with a pictorial rather than abstract design that included gardens and flowers. A delightful example by Mary Ann Richards in the Victoria & Albert Museum in London depicts a house and garden with the flowers inset around the edge, each in individual sprigs of foliage including carnations, this time seen in profile. Techniques of stitching make it difficult to distinguish between pinks and carnations in these samplers, and impossible to guess whether the new varieties that flooded the market in the eighteenth and nineteenth centuries had been seen by these schoolgirls and young women, but the petals of the dianthus are unmistakable whether on an English sampler, an İznik ceramic or an Ottoman wall hanging.

It was this distinctive petal and leaf shape, and the tradition of carnation decoration in medieval and Islamic art, that led William Morris to include the dianthus among his needlework and textile patterns as well as on tiles and furnishings. In 1890 he combined two favourite Elizabethan flowers, the pink and the rose, to create a meandering and intertwining pattern, clearly showing the thin leaf and elongated calyx of the pink with its distinctive serrated petals. Originally available only in colour ranges of pinks and deep rose, it became so popular that it was adapted to polychrome in 1893. Still available via the original company, the wallpaper now comes in a range of colours which early pink fanciers could only dream of, including 'fennel and cowslip', 'indigo', 'eggshell and rose' and the more modern-looking 'Manilla and wine'. It was not until 1905, nine years after Morris's death from overwork, that the company Morris & Co. launched the wallpaper now known as 'Carnation', actually designed by Kate Faulkener (1841–1890), a designer of fabrics and wallpaper. Similar in appearance to the original hand-blocked wallpaper of Morris's lifetime, this was produced by surface roller machines and

Carnations were often included on samplers, as here by Sarah Brignall, 1780.

available in three different colour schemes, the most popular of which appears to have been a faded light green. Perhaps prospective customers were aware of the damning comments by the architect Richard Norman Shaw (1831–1912), who said of Morris's designs:

It is disconcerting, you will admit, when you find that your host and hostess are less noticeable than their wallpapers and their furniture . . . A wallpaper should be a background pure and simple that and nothing more. If there is any pattern at all . . . it ought to be of the simplest kind, quite unobtrusive.[6]

Morris himself was a poet and writer as well as a designer and gardener, and his poem 'The Gilliflower of Gold' envisages a medieval tournament where a knight takes on a series of combatants to defend the honour of his love. The poem commences in a light tone with the start of the tourney, or competition, but becomes increasingly dark with each combat until the end reveals that the woman for which our hero has fought – whether a lover or daughter – has in reality perhaps already been lost, and blood red joins the golden gilliflower.

Whether it was the associations of the florist weavers or the influence of men such as William Morris, who promoted the old cottage garden flowers of the medieval world, the mid-nineteenth and early

William Morris 'Pink and Rose' wallpaper, *c.* 1890.

twentieth centuries saw the carnation and the pink regain popularity not just in the cottage garden but in the newly fashionable 'old-fashioned' garden. In 1827 the rural poet and gardener John Clare recorded in his poem 'The Shepherd's Calendar' – itself a deliberately anachronistic title taken from the Elizabethan poet Edmund Spenser – that farmers' gardens in his Northamptonshire village boasted:

> Snap dragons gaping like to sleeping clowns
> And 'clipping pinks' (which maidens sunday gowns
> Full often wear catch't at by tozing chaps)
> Pink as the ribbons round their snowy caps.

The poem goes on to describe the 'clipping posies' that the maids gather for their swains, which the objects of their affection receive by rising 'to obtain the custom'd kiss'. In 1829 William Cobbett included both the carnation and pink in his book *The English Gardener*, which favoured not only traditional plants but their traditional names. We hear of the lungwort (*Pulmonaria* sp.), mad-wort (*Alyssum saxatile*) and swallow-wort (*Asclepias incarnata*), as well as 'Devil in a Bush', now more commonly known as the rather different 'Love in a Mist' (*Nigella damascena*). Cobbett praises the 'esteemed carnation' which adds scent to colour and is therefore of more worth than the tulip, but saves his real admiration for the 'pretty pink' on which the 'manufacturing people in the north bestow vast pains in propagating and cultivating'.

By the mid-nineteenth century, 'clipping pinks' and the gillyflower carnations in the English cottage gardens were about to move up a class, as they had attracted the eye of the garden writer William Robinson. In the 1860s Robinson, an Irish-born gardener, had been placed in charge of the small collection of English wildflowers at the Regent's Park gardens of the Royal Botanic Society, and in 1870 this experience, combined with a deep-seated hatred of artificiality, led him to write *The Wild Garden*. Robinson included a chapter on 'Carnation, Lily, Iris, and the Nobler Summer Flowers' in this book, encouraging those who had not the skill or the time to grow the florists' flowers to grow instead the 'self'-coloured carnations and pinks in flower beds and borders, liberating them from button-holes and instead enjoying them en masse in the garden. As noted in his book, at the magnificent Shrubland Park in Suffolk Robinson persuaded the owner, Lord de Saumarez, to plant large masses 'to excellent effect' although perhaps rather drifting from his stated 'cottage garden' in both scale and effect. Robinson's own experiments with carnations at his home of Gravetye Manor in Sussex were somewhat devastated in the winter of 1886 when he lost every single plant to rabbits. Undeterred, he put up rabbit netting the following year and replanted 2,000 plants, which he recorded as making a 'fine show' – although they were perhaps beyond the purse of the average cottager.

five
Fit for Royalty: Empresses and Queens

s if divinity were not enough, the carnation has had a long and honourable connection with royalty and aristocracy, both in England and Europe. Agostino del Riccio's 1597 treatise on *Del Giardina di un Re* included sixteen different species or varieties of dianthus that were necessary for the truly royal garden, one which del Riccio imagines will flower every month of the year but will 'indeed [be] very laborious' to keep. He may have modelled his gardening ideas on the Renaissance villas of the Medici, for whom labour was not an issue and who imported rare and beautiful plants to fill their walled gardens and stovehouses. At the villa at Careggi created in 1457 for Cosimo de' Medici the Elder, the scented carnation of the Levant and the lemon trees of Africa were permitted to intrude into a garden otherwise modelled on those of Roman antiquity, with cypress, myrtle, quince and pomegranate. From Italy the carnation travelled north, arriving in England for the reign of Henry VII, but coming into its own with the court of Elizabeth where gillyflowers and roses suffuse poetry and symbolism. Elizabeth herself was not a gardener, leaving it to courtiers such as William Cecil (Lord Burghley), whose gardener John Gerard wrote the important *Herball*. In the frontispiece to this the goddess Flora holds a small dianthus in her hand, possibly the 'Mountain' or 'Deptford Pink' (*Dianthus armeria* or what Gerard knew as *Caryophyllus montanus alba*),[1] but possibly the rather more appropriate 'Virgin' or 'Maidenly Pink' of Gerard. To Flora's left is a distinctively full-petalled red *Dianthus caryophyllus*, while in the centre of the small garden depicted below is a pot of carnations held up by the typical woven work. In the gardens walk a well-dressed man and woman, identified by some as being Lord Burghley and Queen Elizabeth herself, admiring the rare and beautiful plants.

It was Queen Henrietta Maria, ill-fated wife of Charles I, who took to gardening and some sources credit her with raising many carnations and pinks in her own gardens prior to her flight to France,[2] where she could have admired the numerous varieties grown by the French gardener Jean de La Quintinie for his employer Louis XIV at Versailles. Quintinie published a book on the gardens which was later translated into English by John Evelyn, including the rather mournful thought that 'Though the first Bud of a Clove-gilliflower or Carnation is beautiful and Promising, it does not follow thence, that all the rest will be so too,' although Quintinie obviously set high standards for the royal gardens, describing the ideal carnation as 'high and tall, well burnish't and garnish't, well ranged, of a lovely colour, well plumed and displayed, and of a perfectly Velvet-like softness to the Touch'.[3] In the 1690s sufficient numbers of these 'Carnations of Spain' were raised by Quintinie to use as a blanket of bedding in the Versailles gardens, along with sweet williams (*Dianthus barbatus*), cornflowers, wallflowers, lilies and violets;[4] although in 1698 Hans Willem Bentinck, Earl of Portland and William III's ambassador to the French court, was unimpressed, claiming to see none of the flowers that had been so boasted. Bentinck was himself a collector of rarities and obviously difficult to impress. Sarah, Duchess of Marlborough (1660–1744), was another aristocratic flower lover, as well as a close friend and adviser to Queen Anne and chatelaine of the magnificent Blenheim Palace and gardens. The duchess was apparently 'frequently heard to say that nothing gave her so much pleasure as the sight of her Carnations in full bloom, and which she preferred to all the greenhouse plants in her possession'.[5]

The France of Quintinie and Versailles was also the home of the Most Serene House of Condé, a cadet branch of the House of Bourbon which flourished from the mid-sixteenth century to 1830. The greatest of the Condé line was Louis de Bourbon (1621–1686), a military leader who fought most famously at the Battle of Rocroi in 1643 and later at Seneffe against the then prince of Orange (later William III of England) in 1674. Exiled, and later forgiven, by Louis XIV, the Grande Condé shared with the French king a love of flowers, most particularly the carnation, tulip and anemone, which he was said to have personally cared for. At the end of a long life of campaigns, the Grande Condé retired to the Château de Chantilly to spend eleven years devoted to religion and gardens, gathering around him flower collectors and gardeners including Quintinie, and suppliers from distant lands including the Ottoman Empire. His greenhouses and nurseries were supplemented by a 'new flower garden' created in 1682, along with a 'bouquet garden' reserved for creating floral decorations and including, of course, the carnation.

That other great military genius, Napoleon Bonaparte, shared with Condé successes on the battlefield, but it was his lover and first wife Empress Joséphine de Beauharnais (1763–1814) who conquered gardens. Created mistress of some of France's most magnificent gardens at Versailles, Saint-Cloud, the Tuileries and Fontainebleau, Joséphine bought the estate of Malmaison in 1799 as a home for her bourgeoning plant collection. Roses filled the flower beds while plants sent back from military campaigns in Egypt and explorations in Australia and South Africa adorned the hothouses. Napoleon ordered his warship commanders to search all vessels they seized for plants, and, failing to accrue enough in that way, he made arrangements for the ships carrying plants from China back to England for the famous Kennedy nurseries to be allowed free passage on the understanding that Kennedy would also provide roses for Joséphine's gardens. As a result, roses were one of the few items to freely cross the naval blockades of 1810. Joseph Banks, then director of the Royal Botanic Gardens at Kew, also sent rose plants to assist Joséphine in her aim of having every known rose in the Malmaison gardens. The draughtsman and botanical artist Pierre-Joseph

Jean Ranc, *Doña Barbara de Braganza*, 1729, oil on canvas.

Redouté was employed to record the collections at Malmaison in 120 exquisite plates within the twenty-volume work *Jardín de la Malmaison*. The work included specific volumes dedicated just to roses called, rather predictably, *Les Roses*, published 1817–20 – sadly after the death of Joséphine. It was the duty of Joséphine's horticulturalist, Andre Dupont, to provide as many varieties as possible using the same methods of hybridization that had proved so scandalous in the case of the carnation. It has been estimated that at Joséphine's death there were between two hundred and two

ŒILLET REMONTANT

SOUVENIR de la MALMAISON (Laistré)

The big blousy petals of the 'Souvenir de la Malmaison' carnation, from Louis van Houtte's and Charles Lemaire's *Flore des serres et des jardins de l'Europe* (Flowers of the Gardens and Hothouses of Europe, 1857).

hundred and fifty roses at Malmaison, of which only eighty appear in Redouté's work.

In 1843 the rose breeder Jean Béluze created a large, pale pink bourbon rose and decided to name it after Joséphine's famous garden. Rosa 'Souvenir de Malmaison' was born – and with it we can finally cross from the story of the rose back to that of the carnation. Just fourteen years after the birth of the 'Souvenir de Malmaison' rose, a further French nurseryman, M. Laine, created a large pale pink carnation which looked as much like a rose as a carnation and so, the story goes, he named the carnation after the rose. In fact the carnation could have been 'Souvenir de Malmaison' in its own right, as Joséphine was also an ardent cultivator of carnations and picotees, but among all that wealth of roses they have generally been overlooked by history. Malmaison itself fell with the crushing of Napoleon, but the carnation (and the rose) ensured its name lived on in the gardens and nurseries of Europe. Jim Marshall, holder of the National Collection of Malmaison Carnations in his gardens in Suffolk, cites viruses, red spider mite in summer and damping off in winter as the main threats to the malmaison – although the decline from forty cultivars in its heyday to just five now (plus two new cultivars) suggests that the fickle nature of fashion may be the major player in their decline as well as their creation.

Perhaps it was the link with Joséphine that popularized the carnation in France in the early nineteenth century, when Henry Phillips, author of the *Flora historica* (1834), describes

> a whole side of the large *Marché de Halle* perfumed with the fragrance of the carnation bouquets, which *les dames de Halle* were offering to each passenger for a few sous, whilst the agreeable *Marché aux Fleurs* was at the same time covered with these plants in pots, for the purpose of decorating the hotels.[6]

With their large flower and exquisite scent the Malmaison carnations, derived from the 'Tree carnations', went on to become a craze with several 'sports' being created in Scotland, including 'Lady Middleton', who had her origin at Lufness in East Lothian in 1870, and the 'Pink Malmaison' in 1875 in a garden near Musselburgh for the purpose of decorating the courts of the hotels.

Malmaisons are said to be among the most difficult of the carnations to cultivate, with vast glasshouses being devoted to their particular needs, and individuals needing protection from not only the usual hazards of rain, drought, sun, insect attack, or too much or not enough compost and manure, but against 'any check to the plants no matter how slight'.[7] Even then the plant may only produce good-quality blooms for two years, each bloom needing to be carefully wrapped and tended to prevent splitting of the calyx if it is to be of show quality. However, for those who dedicate themselves to the malmaison the reward is a flower up to 6 inches in size on an individual plant reaching up to 5 feet tall. For those with less gardening time on their hands, the perfumers Floris long produced both a perfume and a soap named Malmaison, bringing the scent to everyone. Since the restriction of one of its palette of ingredients, Malmaison has now been reborn as Malmaison Encore – in the words of the advertiser, 'a fragrance for today built on memories of the past'.[8] An apt choice for the garden historian in your life, perhaps?

For all its luxurious massivity the malmaison was not the foremost of carnations among the collections of Queen Charlotte of Mecklenburg-Strelitz (1744–1818). Charlotte, wife of George III, favoured instead the picotee. An amateur botanist and patron of the arts, Charlotte had already given her title to the bird of paradise plant (*Strelitzia reginae*) when it first arrived in England from its native South Africa. The little picotee was a far cry from the bold strelitzia, but among her collection was a rare yellow ground picotee. The picotee (from the French *picoté*, meaning marked with points) is a carnation where the main part of the petal (the [back]ground) is of one colour but the edge or margin is of a different colour – often deep red, rose, scarlet or purple. Ground colours are most often white, but yellow ground picotees were a sought-after favourite in the early

Souvenir de la Malmaison came in a range of pinks and whites in the late 19th century. Botanical print from *L'Illustration horticole* (1887–93).

nineteenth century. Thomas Hogg, in his 1822 treatise on florists' flowers, particularly noted that the picotee, 'with its soft and delicate graces', was often preferred by ladies to the 'gaudy and dazzling beauties' of the carnation, although many florists were wary of them in case they interbred with the carnation and spoilt the line with their more 'playful and unpredictable' irregular spots, dashes and motley colourings. Housed at the royal collection at Frogmore, Queen Charlotte's collection of picotees unfortunately appears to have fallen short of the ideal – an illustration in Hogg's work depicts a sadly blotched and ringed specimen departing in many ways from the ideals of the period. A truer yellow grounded picotee was introduced to the world in 1858 by a Mr Richard Smith of Witney (Oxon), but the parent of most twentieth-century varieties was that introduced by a Mr Perkins in the 1870s and named, somewhat oddly, 'Prince of Orange'.

Aristocracy and royalty were often honoured in the naming of new varieties and one such, 'Baldiston's Queen Adelaide', a flake, frequently appeared in lists of prizewinners in carnation and picotee shows in the early to mid-nineteenth century. It seems to have first come to notice as a 'seedling flake' in July 1830 when it was listed in the Ipswich Flower Show prizewinners entered by a Mr Woollard and recorded as 'afterwards named as Queen Adelaide'. Mr Woollard also entered the winner of the 'Seedling Bizarre' section, with a specimen he later named after another member of royalty, 'Woollard's William the Fourth'. At the Woodbridge (Suffolk) Carnation and Picotée Flower Show, held two days before the Ipswich show, Woollard's 'Miss Bacon' won most beautiful flower of the class, despite the plebeian title, beating competitors such as 'Turner's Princess of Wales' and 'Fletcher's Duchess'. Mr Woollard was described on the occasion as being 'of the Royal William, Ipswich' and was said to have a very good stock of 'Miss Bacon'.[9] In July 1832 a seedling of 'Queen Adelaide' was exhibited at Bedfordshire Horticultural Society Show by a Mr Brinkles, who also took the opportunity of introducing the world to a picotee named 'Brinkle's Delight'.[10] The 'Royal William', from which Mr (William) Woollard hailed, was not as one might have thought a plant nursery, but a public house, to which he had transferred from a similar business at the Whitton Crown in October 1823, and in the *Ipswich Journal* of that date Mr Woollard was described

Dianthus 'Queen of Sheba'.

as a 'florist' who combined the professions of publican and plant retailer. On 23 May 1835 he furthered at least one of those professions when he married Margaret, second daughter of Mr Paterson, a seedsman of Friars Street, Ipswich. Trade in beer and plants must have gone well as he was able to purchase the Royal William public house in 1838, having presumably been only a tenant beforehand. The strange combination of publican and nurseryman is partly solved by the description of the premises at their eventual sale in 1860.[11] The Royal William is described as comprising 'A First rate Tavern and Pleasure Gardens', the latter with 'promenade, bowling green, refreshment booths, lawn, parterres tastefully laid out and planted with shrubs and flowers in rich profusion and covering altogether as an area of four acres (thereabouts) intersected with winding paths'. The gardens themselves were also known as the 'Vauxhall Gardens', presumably in imitation of the more famous London gardens of that name. Also included in the sale were the forcing houses enclosed in high brick walls in which one presumes the 'Queen Adelaide' seedling had first seen light of day. In 1872 the gardens were described in the *Ipswich Journal* on 14 May 1872 as 'Renovated and Improved' by the new proprietor, Leonard Driver. The Royal William was finally demolished in 1998, sadly to make way not for a garden centre but a supermarket.

The real Queen Adelaide (as opposed to her namesake, the flake carnation) was of course the wife of William IV, and queen consort for both the United Kingdom and Hanover, a position for which she had been rapidly chosen in the unseemly scrabble to gain the position of heir presumptive, and the financial settlement that came with it, on the death of George III. William already had ten illegitimate children with a popular actress of the period, but raced to find a suitable bride that would make him, of the king's twelve children, the heir most likely to produce a future legitimate royal line. Adelaide of Saxe-Meiningen (1792–1849), young, innocent and hopefully fertile, seemed an ideal choice, despite the age difference of 27 years, and she was led like a lamb to slaughter. William admitted she was doomed – 'poor dear innocent young creature'.[12] Sadly for all concerned the marriage did not produce the desired result, with no children surviving beyond a few months. Instead Queen Adelaide devoted herself to a variety of interests including her gardens at Windsor and her patronage of several horticultural societies, in return for which she had more than the usual royal share of plants named after her. Dahlias appear to have been her main love and she was patroness of the Salisbury and West of England Royal Dahlia Society,[13] but she also supported the commencement of a new periodical for ladies in 1830, the *Royal Ladies Magazine* by the horticulturalist George Glenny, and employed the royal flower painter, Augusta Withers. At her royal gardens in Windsor, Queen Adelaide (or at least her gardeners) also grew carnations and picotees, of which she was said to have had a very good collection,[14] hopefully including the 'Queen Adelaide' itself.

By the early twentieth century the royal gardeners at Sandringham (Norfolk) included a Mr Thomas H. Cook (FRHS) who boasted, among his other horticultural skills, a specialism in the perpetual carnation. So well known was he that when a book on the cultivation of the carnation was to be published by the New York publishers Frederick A. Stokes, they requested that this English gardener should contribute chapters on what they knew as the 'tree carnation', despite the fact that this type had, in Cook's own estimation, made far more progress in the u.s. than in England, which 'lagged behind' with 'varieties of American origin still holding conspicuously high position in lists sent out by nurserymen of this type'. With the resources of the royal gardens at his disposal, Mr Cook recommended that entire glasshouses be turned over to these carnations, which could then be bedded out in the late spring and might thereby outclass border carnations which had stood out all season. Certainly the gardens at Sandringham were noted under Mr Cook as 'being famous for [their] displays of carnations at every season of the year, including the comparatively sunless months of winter'. Having commenced his carnation career under Edward VII, Mr Cook continued on to deck the borders and glasshouses under Queen Alexandra of Denmark after the death of her husband, Edward VII, in 1910.[15] On her death in 1925, local schoolchildren made a wreath out of 81 carnations, which they had hoped to give to her as a birthday tribute.[16] Queen Alexandra was said to have inherited a love of traditional flowers from her own mother, Queen Louise of Denmark, who had the gardens of her palace at Freidensborg laid out with peonies, pinks, carnations and sweet williams. She also had a 'Norwegian Garden' with one hundred figures in national costume.[17]

Although never to be queen, Wallis Simpson, lover and downfall of Edward VIII, combines royalty, politics and carnations in one bouquet. In 1936, with the Second World War just three years in the future, the then king, Edward, was torn between his love for the American divorcee Wallis Simpson and his dynastic responsibilities. The couple spent the summer at country houses with friends sympathetic to their match, moving in court and ambassadorial circles. Among those ambassadors was the German representative Joachim von Ribbentrop, future foreign minister in the Nazi regime that was to follow. It was a year of scandal and upheaval for court and country. By the end of the year Edward had abdicated, becoming the Duke of Windsor, while his lover was now his wife and the Duchess of Windsor. In 1941, with Britain reeling from Blitz and blockade, the duke and duchess were enjoying three days of relaxation at Palm Beach, Florida, having fled from a war-torn Europe, escaping France through Spain and Portugal and staying one step ahead of, but not actively fleeing, the fascist host. What they did not know was that the American president Franklin Delano Roosevelt, deeply suspicious of the couple's relationship with the Nazi leaders, had instigated an FBI intelligence exercise to gather information on their past. The investigating officers interviewed one Father Odo, a Benedictine monk who before the war had been the Duke of Württemberg, a minor member of the German royal family with connections to Queen Mary, Edward's mother. Father Odo told them that in 1936 Ribbentrop had been the lover of Wallis Simpson at the same time

Carnations being packed in Britain for the royal wedding of Princess Elizabeth and Philip Mountbatten in 1947.

Carnations for the royal wedding exhibited as bunches prior to packing.

as she had been the lover of Edward VIII. According to Father Odo, the evidence for the sexual liaison between Ribbentrop and Simpson was confirmed by Ribbentrop sending her seventeen carnations every day that summer, seventeen being the number of times they had made love. Whatever the truth of this (and other sources suggested only one bouquet of an unspecified number of flowers, while others mentioned roses), the Duke and Duchess of Windsor were known to favour the Nazi regime. On 13 September 1940 a memo confirmed that the duchess was passing information to her erstwhile German lover about British and French official activities, and the duke and duchess were banished to the Bahamas, where it was thought they could do little harm or be in receipt of no useful information for their German contacts – and where carnations would be in short supply.[18] Fortunately, by the time of the wedding of the future Queen Elizabeth II to Lieutenant Philip Mountbatten RN (later the Duke of Edinburgh) in 1947, carnations were again available in greater supply both in England and America, where many of the wedding blooms came from. The British Carnation Society was able to decorate each table with pink and white carnations to be admired by the guests, including the then king and queen of Denmark. Notable by their absence, however, were the Duke and Duchess of Windsor. Perhaps, given the carnations at the tables, this was just as well.

One final royal connection could fit also into art, as it brings together again the aristocratic ladies of Europe and that foremost botanical artist Pierre-Joseph Redouté, who recorded the rare and beautiful plants at Malmaison for Empress Joséphine. Princess Louise Marie Eugénie Adélaïde d'Orléans was the sister of Louis-Philippe I, king of France from 1830 to 1848. Known as Princess Adélaïde, her early life was one of upheaval as revolution forced the family to flee, before returning in 1814 to live in the Palais Royale. As an unmarried woman with a strong intellect and political feeling, she became the centre of a 'salon' for artists and intellectuals who supported opposition to the Bourbon regime, but Princess Adélaïde also found time

In 18th-century Europe, the carnation was associated with genteel ladies, and pictured as such in this German image.

to take lessons from Redouté, eventually becoming one of his most talented pupils. Probably instructed privately in her Palais apartments, Princess Adélaïde and of course her tutor would have had access to a wealth of flowers and plants from the gardens. Only a handful of her paintings survive, dating to the 1820s, but among them is a posy containing the most exquisite deep purple carnation depicted from the rear to allow the detail of its calyx to be seen. It nestles among asters, harebells, violas and a wild rose, most probably dating the painting to July. Drops of water stand on the rose as a moment is caught in time betwixt revolution and royalty. Also taking lessons from Redouté in the 1820s was Princess Louise d'Orléans, daughter of Louis-Philippe and niece of Princess Adélaïde. Although not as accomplished an artist as her aunt, a greater number of her pieces survive, most of which are of individual specimen flowers. Among these is a single carnation stalk with two flowers. Rich raspberry-pink, with darker fine stripes and dashes, it is at once simple and luxurious and easily rivals the roses seen in so many paintings by Redouté's aristocratic pupils, and for which French royalty had been famous.[19]

six

A Rainbow of Pinks

Of sev'ral hue I sev'ral Garments wear,
Nor can the Rose her self with me compare:
. . . The very Croesus I of colours am
ABRAHAM COWLEY, 'July-flower', in *Six Books of Plants*
(1668)

P assion, purity, undying love, or rejection and disappointment: the colour of a carnation holds the key to understanding the message and the emotion. As with many flowers, the symbolism of carnations was first attributed in the medieval period, when illiteracy of the masses necessitated emphasis on wordless interpretation, but colours were limited. The Victorians added new colours and further meanings and nuances, many of them sentimental or sexual. Pride of place here must be given to the white carnation, synonymous with purity and luck, innocence, pure love and lovely faithfulness. The colour pink signals appreciation, mother's love and perfect happiness, but with greater depth of colour comes the growth of sexual passion. Light red is for admiration, pride and friendship tempered with respect, unlike the deep dark red where passion aches for its subject in a wordless hidden affection and a bursting heart. The Baron de Ponsort wrote that the red carnation was 'the mysterious confidante of the most secret thoughts, the discrete interpreter of the feelings that our mouths dare not utter'.[1] Deep purples, only available with hybrid breeding or artificial colouring, appropriately

The gloriously orange 'Apricot Self' carnation, 1888.

suggest unpredictability and changefulness. Fantasy is appropriately restricted to the unlikely mauve carnation, never to be combined in a wedding bouquet with the yellow carnation of disappointment, rejection and disdain. The unpredictable striped carnation was held by the Victorians to mean 'you are absent' – a strangely contradictory message given that the Paisley loom weavers who treasured these cultivars were famous for giving constant attention to their charges.

The story of love starts with the hopeful pink carnation, in solid colour rather than striped, which might already impart a coming refusal. Now often thought of as the cheap and easy option, with overtones of long-lasting bouquets purchased at supermarket checkouts and garage forecourts, the pink carnation or pink originally echoed the pink traditionally hidden among the bride's clothing, to be discovered by an amorous searching bridegroom after the ceremony was complete. Popular in European wedding tradition, the colour of the dianthus hidden in the wedding clothes does not appear to have been specified, although the original 'flesh' colour might seem appropriate, or the dark red carnation of passion, rather than the virginal and innocent white so often used in bridal bouquets in the twentieth century, themselves perhaps remnants of the more passionate single flower. The maiden pink, or *Dianthus deltoides*, cousin to the garden pink, may also be a candidate for the bridegroom's search. Its name refers to the blushing pink colour of its petals and it has long been associated with simple pleasures. Native to Europe, the maiden pink is a perennial that flowers for several months over the summer, making it suited to the wedding season. It includes modern varieties with names such as 'Pixie Star' that take one straight back to the fairy world of Titania, Oberon and Puck in *A Midsummer Night's Dream*, replete with Bottom the weaver transformed with the head of a donkey and in love with the fairy queen. The always lusty poet Robert Herrick (1591–1674) may have been referring to the tradition of searching for the pink when he penned his seventeenth-century poem 'The Carnation':

> Stay while ye will, or go,
> And leave no scent behind ye:
> Yet trust me, I shall know
> The place where I may find ye.
>
> Within my Lucia's cheek,
> (Whose livery ye wear)
> Play ye at hide or seek,
> I'm sure to find ye there.

Herrick had been a cleric in his early life and, after the restoration of Charles II, returned to his calling as the vicar of Dean Prior in Devonshire. His appearance in the pulpit after becoming famous for poems such as 'To the Virgins' and 'The Poet Loves a Mistress, but Not to Marry' must have put a carnation blush on the faces of

overleaf: Pure white carnations and pinks are associated with purity.

some of his congregation. Back in the rather more staid twentieth century, the one-year anniversary of a wedding is often traditionally celebrated with a bouquet of carnations, which represents lasting love, along with the top tier of the wedding cake, which if it survived the year was said to be a lucky omen.

A modern bridegroom will not await an evening romp with his newly beloved to display his love of the carnation. Instead he, his best man and most male guests will be decked out with white carnation buttonholes, or more correctly boutonnières, at all but the most informal of weddings. The boutonnière has a history all of its own dating to the late eighteenth century, when a portrait by Gainsborough of a Captain William Wade appeared replete with a small flower posy affixed to his scarlet frockcoat. Wade was the master of ceremonies at Bath's Assembly Rooms between 1769 and 1777 and his fashionable clothes and delicate but substantial posy were to be seen by all the *beau-monde* both in reality and in the painting, which was commissioned by the owners of the Assembly Rooms and hung there long after Wade himself had moved on. Wade's posy could not be inserted through a lapel buttonhole because nothing of the sort then existed, although the inspiration for such might have been seen in the informal 'opening' of the riding coat, allowing the top quarter to lie to one side. It was the introduction of the frockcoat in around 1830 with its double breasting and multitudinous buttons and ancillary buttonholes that permitted the threading through of a stem, and in 1838 the French writer and dandy Jules-Amédée Barbey d'Aurevilly (1808–1889) recorded, 'I sacrifice a rose each evening to my buttonhole.' By the mid-nineteenth century, the arrival of the Deeside or Tweedside coat, with its 'ghillie' or shirt collar style, frequently resulted in the turning down of the top button below the collar to display the tie, and – hey presto! – the buttonhole for the 'buttonhole' was finally achieved, along with the otherwise inexplicable 'notch' to the lapel. A stitched loop on the rear of the turnback additionally allowed the stem of the flower(s) to be held in place once inserted through the buttonhole. On a high-class suit jacket, the buttonhole was often made larger than any real button would need so that the calyx of a more bulbous flower, such as the carnation, could be fully inserted. Pinning the flower to the lapel is regarded as both unsightly and damaging to the jacket itself, particularly in the case of a silk dinner jacket, and should never be done.

The only surviving portraits of the sacrificial dandy Barbey d'Aurevilly depict him distressingly *sans* boutonnière. However, when the French painter James Tissot sketched the artist-collector Frederic, Lord Leighton (1830–1896), for a *Vanity Fair* cartoon in 1872, he placed him in a languid pose wearing black tails and a white dress shirt and sporting a posy of flowers including carnations. Entitled *A Sacrifice to the Graces*, the full-length portrait conveyed the urbane elegance of Leighton, who entertained lavishly and gathered the artistic world around him at his home in Holland Park. Self-promotion was vital to Leighton in his pursuit of sales, but his languid style did not at first inspire those outside the artistic community to follow his fashion for the boutonnière, especially when the flower was seen in the same location of men of such 'dubious' character as Oscar Wilde, who was of course to lay claim to the very special green carnation. Nevertheless, carnations increasingly made appearances and by the Edwardian era they were a *sine qua non* of the well-dressed man about town.

In 1906 a portrait of the dapper William Hall Walker 'dressed for the races' boasted a salmon-coloured carnation appropriate for daywear, while two years later *Vanity Fair* again presented the fashionable but mature racegoer in the form of a Mr P. P. Gilpin depicted with a red carnation so enlarged as to totally obscure not only the buttonhole but the entire lapel. However, it was the appearance of the same flower in the buttonhole of HRH Prince of Wales in the 1930s that led to a rush to copy the aristocratic style on both sides of the Atlantic. Debonair, immaculately dressed for all occasions and setting a new fashion in 'midnight blue' evening wear, the Prince of Wales wore a white carnation with both day and evening wear. Referring back to the meaning of flowers, its message 'Alas my poor heart' was perhaps not the best choice for the abdicated king (shortly to become the Duke of Windsor) when he married Wallis Simpson in 1937. Nevertheless, the white carnation became identified with 'Windsor style' and was taken up by both the elegant and the dashing, including Fred Astaire and Gary Cooper. Only Cary Grant stood out from its purity and aristocracy with a passionately red carnation, while Douglas Fairbanks Jr appears to have dithered between the two. The red or even 'scarlet' carnation was also sported by a man who played onscreen cads more often than clean-cut heroes: the appearance of the actor Terry-Thomas in houndstooth suit, with cigarette holder and bright red carnation, spoke volumes – mainly words of warning. The large single bloom, accompanied by its small ferny backing, was sold through florists and also on the streets, with flower girls still a common sight in the 1920s and an entire carnation industry set up as a result of the demand for the aristocratic style. Vast fields of carnations became a common sight in parts of America and Italy, and carnations for boutonnières were grown under glass in England both commercially and in country house gardens, where they were produced for the aristocratic owners and their guests.

A play called *The White Carnation* by R. C. Sherriff (better known for his First World War play, *Journey's End*) draws on the button-holed formality of the Second World War upper-middle class for its spectral tale of loss and anxiety never quite resolved. The wearer of the eponymous carnation is as ghostly as the petals, having died six years prior to the setting of the play, when a V-1 flying bomb killed his wife and their dinner party guests. Also associated with dignity through war and suffering, in the Netherlands white carnations were associated with Prince Bernhard. The prince wore one during the Second World War in coded support for the resistance movement, and in a gesture of defiance some of the Dutch population did the same. After the war the white carnation became a sign of the prince, veterans and remembrance of the resistance.

By the early twentieth century the carnation in the lapel had expanded its following both socially and geographically to include

Boris Kustodiev, *Ivan Bilibin*, 1914, oil on canvas. Men in the arts often sported the red carnation rather than the white — signalling passion for their work.

the cottage-dwelling classes as far afield as Australia. 'The Pink Carnation' by Henry Lawson (1867–1922), written 1905–10, records a period of Lawson's life when, despite being one of Australia's most popular poets and balladeers, he had fallen into depression and alcoholism. Destitute from poor royalty contracts and hounded by his ex-wife for child maintenance, Lawson ended up in Darlinghurst

Gaol where the meagre rations further weakened his constitution. His life was eventually saved by Mrs Bryers, a fellow poet and woman of independent means who took Lawson in and nursed him through the next twenty years of his life. The poem looks back to happier days and needs to be read in the ballad style of the era in which its pink carnation sets it:

I may walk until I'm fainting, I may write until I'm blinded,
I might drink until my back teeth are afloat,
But I can't forget my ruin and the happy days behind it,
When I wore a pink carnation in my coat.

Oh, I thought that time could conquer, and I thought my
heart would harden,
But it sends a sudden lump into my throat,
When I think of what I have been, and the cottage and the
garden,
When I wore a pink carnation in my coat.

God forgive you, girl, and bless you! Let no line of mine
distress you –
I am sorry for the bitter lines I wrote;
But remember, and think kindly, for we met and married
blindly,
When I wore a pink carnation in my coat.

From love and marriage (happy or sad), the red carnation moves us on seamlessly to revolution and war. A military coup does not often end bloodlessly, or a dictator fall to a flower, but the Portuguese revolution of 25 April 1974 did just that. The revolution commenced as a coup organized by the Movimento das Forças Armadas but was taken up by the populace to become an unanticipated general rising against the established regime of the Estado Novo, or New State, an authoritarian right-wing regime. The rising was expected to be a bloody conflict, its commencement marked by a coded message of the playing of a traditional folk song on the Portuguese radio, and as the military swung into action at the sound of the song, radio bulletins urged the population to stay safe indoors. Instead, thousands of people took to the streets, supporting and encouraging the military. Gathering in the central flower market of Lisbon, richly stocked with carnations in preparation for May Day celebrations, the citizens placed flowers in the gun barrels of the men and tanks as the dictator Caetano gave way to the inevitable without the expected carnage taking place. Following this *Revuluçâon dos Cravos* (Carnation Revolution), red carnations were used to symbolize Portugal's slow return to democracy, and now appear in posters and on marches marking the anniversary of revolution every 25 April, on what is known as Freedom Day.

On May Day, the red carnation again plays a part in worldwide marches and demonstrations in support of socialism. Its identification with the workers' struggle is claimed by some to date back to the original May Day celebrations of the Middle Ages when the workers had days off, but a more probable association between the carnation and the socialist cause dates from the mid-1880s when trade unionists in America wore red carnations to identify themselves with the eight union leaders convicted of incitement to riot during the Haymarket affair, or Haymarket massacre. A mass meeting between union members and police at the McCormick Harvesting Machine Company in Chicago led to riot and mayhem after a bomb was exploded. Unlike the Carnation Revolution ninety years later, this did not end peacefully and seven policemen and between four and eight civilians were killed. The impact on trade unionism in America was to be long lasting. As socialism's struggles spread across the world, so did the symbolism of the red carnation, and in Italy, Austria and the states that made up the former Yugoslavia the carnation now makes an annual appearance.

The trade union leaders may not have realized that in taking the sign of the carnation they were following in the very different

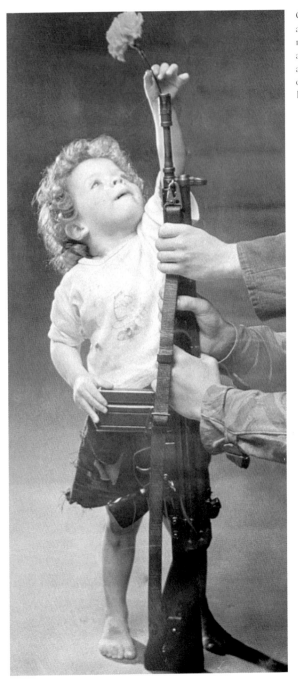

Child placing a carnation in a muzzle, an image associated with anti-war posters of the Portuguese Revolution, 1974.

In June 2013 Turkish people came to Istanbul's Taksim Square with red carnations to commemorate those who had died during the recent protests.

May Day military parades in East Berlin in 1975.

footsteps of the French general and politician Georges Ernest Jean-Marie Boulanger (1837–1891). Nicknamed Général Revanche for his aggressive nationalism (known in French as *revanchisme*), Boulanger won a series of elections through the 1870s and '80s, and was at one time thought to be heading for a popular dictatorship. His 'Boulangist' supporters called for revenge for the Franco-Prussian defeat of France in the previous decade and were mainly drawn from the conservative and royalist elements of French society and political life. Boulanger himself had taken part in the actions that had crushed the Paris Commune in 1871 and actively supported the return of the monarchy. Boulanger's supporters took the red carnation as their identifying emblem even after the fall of their hero and his eventual suicide in October 1891. Boulanger was depicted in newsprint committing suicide by the tomb of his mistress, Madame de Bonnemains, in the Ixelles cemetery (Belgium), some depictions including the carnation in the wreaths. The image was used again as an advertising poster for a play by Georges Fagot based on Boulanger's life, entitled *Le Legende de l'oeillet*, while a satirical board game based on his life and published in *Le Figaro* in 1889 depicts Boulanger and his supporters each with a large red carnation in their buttonhole.

In Russia (and until recently large parts of what is now the former Soviet Union), the Revolution of 1917 is celebrated with red carnations. Every 7 November sees parades and speeches in memory of the 'Great October Socialist Revolution', which incidentally shifted ten days into November with the Soviet adoption of the Gregorian calendar in 1918. As part of the celebrations, Soviet workers carry balloons and carnations in the deep red of socialism and communism, and carnation bouquets are awarded to party functionaries. In 1965 a Russian postage stamp featuring the red carnation of socialism was released, giving a splash of colour to communications. Postcards and greetings cards bearing the date, flag and a carnation are frequently exchanged. Were there to be a 'scent of the day' to linger over the staged performances it would undoubtedly be the *Krasnaya Moskva* (Red Moscow), a rich carnation-based perfume and

The play *La Legende de l'oeillet* by Georges Fagot was popular in the aftermath of the suicide of General Boulanger.

one of the few that were available to the Soviet populace prior to the easing of importation restrictions.

Rather confusingly, the scarlet carnation is also the state flower of Ohio, not known for its communist tendencies. The choice was made in honour of the u.s. President and Ohio Governor William McKinley, who was said to wear the carnation in his buttonhole every day from his initial bid for the United States Congress in 1876 until

Sean Connery as
James Bond in
Goldfinger (1964).

his assassination in 1901. Levi Lambourn, McKinley's opponent in
his 1876 campaign, was a horticulturalist and had developed a red
carnation suitable for use as a boutonnière, generously giving one to
McKinley. McKinley wore it during the debates and, winning the
campaign, felt it was a good luck token. Once in the Oval Office he
also kept a spray of the carnations, offering them to visitors. Legend
has it that while shaking hands in a greeting line-up at the Pan-
American Exposition in Buffalo, New York, McKinley gave away his
red carnation to a small girl in the Temple of Music. Moments later
the anarchist Leon Czolgosz stepped out of the crowd and shot the
president. McKinley died a few days later on 14 September 1901, a
date now marked every year as Red Carnation Day in Ohio.

С праздником
ВЕЛИКОГО ОКТЯБРЯ!

The 1917 Russian Revolution is still commemorated with carnations on postcards and used in parades.

If red is associated with communism and socialism, then for some a lean to the left may be marked in shades of pink. The term 'pink' or 'pinko' was first used as a description of someone with left-wing political views in the 1920s. Referring to followers of the progressive Senator Robert La Follette, the *Wall Street Journal* concluded they were 'visionaries, ne'er-do-wells, and parlor pinks'.[2] Although the *Journal* was probably referring to the effeteness and sensitivity of soul traditionally symbolized by pinks (most especially in France), *Time* magazine then went on to coin the word 'pinko' to refer to a political stance in 1925. Although not directly referring to the flower, the connection with the red carnation makes the fantasy of these 'visionaries' holding aloft pink pinks rather attractive.

Students of the University of Oxford vary the colour of carnation they wear not according to their political stance, but according to their progress through their studies. Examination regulations traditionally dictate that every year both male and female students should be attired in subfusc (from the Latin for dark brown), comprising academic gowns, dark suit and bow ties. In the first year of examinations this is accompanied by a white carnation, for the final year a red carnation and for any examinations in between a pink carnation. The change

William McKinley's assassination in 1901 gave rise to memorial cards, such as this one for National Carnation Day.

A Favorite in Flowers

THE CARNATION — State Flower of Ohio

DIXIE BELLE

Qualities people prefer are the qualities that make a favorite. Take Dixie Belle, for instance. Here's gin whose exquisite bouquet and bright, clear-cut flavor are distilled into every drop from selected herbs, fruits and berries and choice grain neutral spirits. You'll instantly recognize its marked superiority with your first taste . . . the taste that makes DIXIE BELLE a favorite everywhere.

A Favorite in **GIN**

90 Proof • Distilled from 100% Grain Neutral Spirits • CONTINENTAL DISTILLING CORPORATION, PHILADELPHIA, PA.

The red carnation of the state flower of Ohio here used to advertise Dixie Belle gin.

from white to red over the years is said (almost certainly apocryphally) to be a result of the carnation being kept in a pot of red ink between one exam and the next and thus by the final exams turning red. No such floricultural pride attends examinations at the University of Cambridge, which might be good news for hayfever sufferers.

Another occasion on which a change in colour denotes the passage of time is Mother's Day in the United States and Canada, now

MOTHERS' DAY

White flowers we mingle
with red everywhere,
Setting this day apart
from the rest;
So mothers who live, may
with those over there,
Be honored as of all friends
the best.

usually held on the second Sunday in May. Ann Jarvis, who started the tradition of Mother's Day, originally chose the white carnation because she wanted the flower to represent the purity of a mother's love, but the symbolism has evolved over time, and now a red carnation may be worn if one's mother is alive and a white one if she has died. In Korea, where the sexes share equally in Parents' Day on 8 May, both red and pink carnations are worn and some parents wear a corsage of carnations. During the era of the People's Republic of Poland, the country celebrated Women's Day rather than Mother's Day, but still the carnation featured, together with toiletries and other small gifts that were hard to acquire under the communist system.

Although reds, pinks and whites are the most common and traditional colours for the dianthus, the carnation's mutability in breeding and its ability to absorb colours through water (similar to the flamingo's change of colour through its eating habits) have added the most unlikely colourings to the natural 'carne' or flesh tones of nature's original, producing everything from salmon through to yellow, mauve and even green. Carnations do not naturally produce the pigment delphinidin, so abundant in the delphinium, but the perfume house Roger & Gallet captured the scent of the impossible when it launched its Oeillet Bleu in 1937. The heady combination of cinnamon carnation mingled with clove, bay and vanilla captured pre-war decadence – velvet, heavy but spicy sweet. Its heaviness and distinctive allure marked it as the perfume worn by women wanting to attract men. Its passing in 1976 marked a shift in the role of women and the battle of the sexes, leaving the way open to a cocktail of the same name, which was perhaps less temptingly sensual. Anyone fortunate enough to track down a bottle of Roger & Gallet's Oeillet Bleu will be in for a surprise: it was marketed with an image not of a blue carnation but of a cornflower (*bleuet* in French). That the cornflower traditionally symbolizes delicacy and timidity and stands in place of the red poppy of remembrance for France's war dead only adds to the confusion. Mauve carnations, until recently only available through the 'watering' technique, are also associated with funerals in France, given as a sign of sympathy or condolence to the bereaved, and unsurprisingly the carnation generally is sometimes seen as a symbol of bad luck in France.

Another artificial colour – green – was used by the playwright and wit Oscar Wilde. Subverting the socially exclusive association of the white carnation and the boutonnière, Wilde arranged for an actor at the first night's performance of *Lady Windermere's Fan* to wear a green dyed carnation. He sent his friends boutonnières of the same colour and created an instant clique. When asked for the reason behind his choice he famously declared, 'nothing whatever, but that is just what nobody will guess', but green's association with the decadence of absinthe (a bright green liqueur) and the temperament of the artist would prove sufficient explanation to those in the know.

In 1894 a book was anonymously published whose characters were said to be based closely on Oscar Wilde and his lover Lord Alfred Douglas; it was titled, inevitably, *The Green Carnation*. The hero (or anti-hero), Lord Reginald Hastings, is introduced to the reader in the first line as he 'slipped a green carnation into his evening coat, fixed it in its place with a pin and looked at himself in the long glass'. Reggie, the reader is informed, adores himself as a consequence of his love of beauty, delights in his own genius and chooses his friends for their bad reputations as much as for their charm. The 'white flower of a blameless life was too inartistic to have any attraction for him'. The choice of the green carnation for Reggie is explained by his belief that 'Art showed the way to Nature and [he] worshipped the abnormal with all the passion of his impure and subtle youth.' The green motif is continued in the fictional naming of his close friend, 'Mr Esmé Amarinth'. It is Esmé Amarinth who represents Oscar Wilde, in whose after-dinner conversation 'jokes, nude, no longer clad in the shadowy garments of more or less conventional propriety, danced like bacchanals through the conversation, and kicked up heels to fire even the weary men of society'. A review of the book in *The Observer* newspaper at the time of its publication commented that 'nothing so impudent, so bold or so delicious has been printed these many years' and Wilde himself was forced to write to the *Pall Mall Gazette* refuting the claim that he was the author of *The Green Carnation*. Wilde admitted that 'I invented that magnificent flower. But with the middle-class and mediocre book that usurps its strangely beautiful name I have, I need hardly say, nothing whatsoever to do. The flower is a work of Art, the book is not'.[3] Whatever the merits or otherwise of the book, or the green carnation as a work of art or nature, Robert Hichens's fictional exposé led to the trial and eventual conviction of the wit who formed its focus, resulting in two years' hard labour and his fall from society.

The green carnation was not, however, lost sight of. *Bitter Sweet*, the 1929 musical by the suitably suave Noël Coward, included a song titled 'We All Wear a Green Carnation'. Not a fan of Oscar Wilde

A green carnation produced with artificial dye.

Oscar Wilde, sporting the carnation for which he was to become infamous.

– in his diaries Coward wrote, 'I have read the Oscar Wilde letters and have come to the reluctant conclusion that he was one of the silliest, most conceited and unattractive characters that ever existed'[4] – Coward nevertheless captured the tone of the world-weary Wilde in his lyrics:

Pretty boys, witty boys,
Too too too
Lazy to fight stagnation
Haughty boys, naughty boys,
All we do
Is to pursue sensation
The portals of society are always opened wide
The world our eccentricity condones

a note of quaint variety we're certain to provide
We dress in very decorative tones
Faded boys, jaded boys
Womankind's
Gift to a bulldog nation
In order to distinguish us from less enlightened minds
We all wear a green carnation.

The 'green carnation' thus became even more firmly associated with the 'outing' of homosexuality in the 1930s than it had been in the 1890s, although Coward himself never formally 'came out', declaring when encouraged to do so that 'There are still a few old ladies in Worthing who don't know.' A Soho club now bears the name of the verdant dianthus, continuing its reputation for disreputableness. Since 2010 there has been a Green Carnation Prize for LGBT literature (in association with Foyles bookshop). The prize is open to all LGBT writers and is destined to cause confusion to any horticulturalist browsing for information on a new strain. Oscar Wilde's championing of the green carnation may also lead to some political confusion, as the flower, 'reborn' as an artificial creation, has recently become associated, alongside all other things green, with St Patrick's Day and is worn on that day by Irish people all over the world. In 2015 the organizers of the New York St Patrick's Day Parade were divided over the inclusion of gay and same-sex groups at the Irish celebrations – a shame as the celebrants could otherwise have claimed the right to wear two green carnations.

Which leaves us with the yellow of the otherwise replete rainbow of carnations. The pure yellow dianthus has been sought after over the centuries, and seemingly discovered, lost and discovered again in different varieties, each time being declared yellower than that which went before. It is now a common sight in carnation bouquets but in the hierarchy of carnation symbolism, yellow, being a latecomer to the scene, has been left with the bitterness of 'rejection' or the rather alarming message, 'You have disappointed me' – not something one usually expects to read in a gift of flowers. Finally, the use of the word 'carnation' as commonly used in the sixteenth century to describe the colour of other pink flowers, and even fabrics, has surprisingly stayed with us despite the fact that it could now denote any of the colours of the rainbow.

seven

A Picture of Pink
ᘏ

I see a cut glass vase, sitting supreme
upon the polished surface
with rose, carnation and dahlias,
near by a collection of love
HARRY J. HORSMAN, from 'The Old Jam Jar' (2012)

In a late summer afternoon in 1885 in the English Cotswold
village of Broadway, the artist John Singer Sargent commenced
a painting that was to take him two years to complete. Capturing
the warm glow of the dying sun in the garden of his artist friend
Francis David Millet, Sargent composed his subject of two young
girls lighting Chinese lanterns against a backdrop of lilies, roses and
carnations. Sargent had taken the inspiration for the painting from
the rows of Chinese lanterns he had seen during a boating exped-
ition on the Thames at Pangbourne that year with the American
artist Edwin Austin Abbey. The project had a somewhat unsettled
start, being commenced in the gardens of the house rented by Millet
at Broadway and then, when he moved, at his new gardens at Russell
House in the same village. At first the girl in the picture was to be
Millet's daughter Katherine (aged five) but her hair colour was
'wrong' and Sargent replaced her with Polly (aged seven) and Dolly
(aged eleven), daughters not of Millet but of the illustrator Frederick
Barnard. The two girls were posed among a wealth of garden flowers
and shown concentrating on lighting their lanterns. Carnations, in

Dark crimson against their grey leaves in contrast to the light pink roses,
the carnations of the title surround the two girls in John Singer Sargent's
Carnation, Lily, Lily, Rose, 1885–6, oil on canvas.

red and white, stood in almost implausible floral richness around
the feet of the girls while lilies towered over them and roses framed
the image.

Over the two summers during which the life-size painting occupied him, Sargent worked on it for only a few moments each day,
waiting for the ideal light with its perfect mauve tint to illuminate
the scene. His friend Edmund Gosse recorded Sargent's working
method as the correct light would start to appear:

Instantly, [Sargent] took up his place at a distance from the canvas, and at a certain notation of the light ran forward over the lawn with the action of a wag-tail, planting at the same time rapid dabs of paint on the picture, and then retiring again, only, with equal suddenness, to repeat the wag-tail action. All this occupied but two or three minutes, the light rapidly declining, and then, while he left the young ladies to remove his machinery, Sargent would join us again, so long as the twilight permitted, in a last turn at lawn tennis.[1]

As the blooms inevitably faded they were replaced with new ones, but what exactly were they? The roses have been suggested as being the newly bred 'Cecile Brunner', pink and fluffy, the lilies may be the *Lilium giganteum*, but the carnations remain unnamed. Given the date of the painting and the length of the stems, they may be one of the more than fifty varieties of 'tree carnation' that were then available, although their planting out in the garden among the grasses (if not purely a stage-managed set-up) would argue instead for a border or garden carnation. Unnamed though they are, they do boast the lead flower of the title that Sargent chose for his work, *Carnation, Lily, Lily, Rose*. The title was taken from a popular song of the period by the Corsican/English Joseph Mazzinghi, 'Ye Shepherds Tell Me', which ran:

> Ye Shepherds tell me,
> Tell me have you seen,
> Have you seen My Flo-ra pass this way? . . .
> A wreath around her head,
> Around her head she wore
> Carnation, lilly, lilly, rose;
> And in her hand a crook she bore,
> And sweets her breath compose.

After two years of struggling with the light, the growing children and the dying flowers, Sargent began to regret his dedication to one particular light, and took to calling the picture 'Darnation Silly Silly Pose', but it became his most famous canvas, endlessly reproduced, and through its title, the most famous carnation art.

Sargent's carnations may remain unidentified, but those of the more botanically minded artists that preceded him did not lurk in such anonymity. *Dianthus chinensis*, later to play a vital role in the development of the perpetual flowering carnation, was depicted by Georg Dionysius Ehret in 1764 in a delicate watercolour of a species native to the faraway regions of China, Korea and Mongolia. The depiction looks fragile with spindly leaves and small red and white flowers atop elongated stems. In reality it is a perennial plant which makes its home in forest margins and grasslands, along mountain streams and in the steppes of Mongolia. It has given rise to many cultivars in China but Ehret is not specific as to which he depicted. In 1764 the plant was a relative newcomer to Europe, the first seeds having been sent from China to France in around 1705 and the first flowers recorded in Paris from 1719. Ehret was the son of a gardener and himself a keen botanist and entomologist, as well as a botanic artist and teacher of flower painting. From the 1730s he had lived in London, painting exotics at the Chelsea Physic Garden and by the 1760s, when *Dianthus chinensis* came to his attention, he was a fellow of the Royal Society. He had carried out illustrations for Philip Miller's *The Gardener's Dictionary* as well as *Hortus Kewensis* for William Aiton, recording the new plants arriving at Kew from around the world. Chinese plants and 'Chinese-style' gardens became fashionable in mid-eighteenth-century Europe, most particularly France and England, and Chinese 'kiosks' and elaborately painted Chinese temples and teahouses would have greeted the small 'China Pink' at gardens such as Woodside House, Berkshire. The planting in these gardens was often less than geographically strict, as fashion for rococo motifs overlapped with that for chinoiserie, leaving owners in a frenzy of indecision over the inclusion of plants from the Americas. For others the terms 'Chinese', 'Japanese' and even 'Indian' became interchangeable. Indeed *Dianthus chinensis* was also known as *Dianthus sinensis* and the 'Indian Pink', or even the 'Empire Pink'. Specializing in the recording of such gardens in England were father and son artists Thomas Robins the Elder and the Younger. It was Thomas Robins the Elder who painted an image of Woodside Gardens in the late 1750s, including on the painted 'frame' a honeysuckle, *Lathyrus* sp., primula and, of course, an 'Indian Pink'.

In comparison to the delicate *oeillet de Chine* or *Dianthus chinensis*, the blossoming *Dianthus caryophyllus* captured by fellow eighteenth-century artist Pierre-Joseph Redouté is rose-like, with large rich petals and broader leaves. Redouté often included carnations in his popular paintings of flower 'posies', but for his collected water-colours entitled *Choix des plus belles fleurs et des plus beaux fruits* (Choice of the most beautiful flowers and fruits) he chose a flower with petals striped in purple pinks on a white ground. Published in Paris in the years 1827–30, the volumes represent the very best flowers of the period and the exquisite skill of the man known as 'the Raphael of flowers'. In this, his last great work before his death at the age of eighty in 1840, Redouté explained that he personally had chosen the plants and flowers for inclusion:

Thomas Robins the Elder, *Chinese Pavilion in an English Garden*, 18th century, watercolour and gouache on paper. Woodside in Berkshire: one of the many gardens that included decoration in chinoiserie style.

Enlightened by experience and encouraged by extremely flattering pleas of naturalists and painters from my own country as well as from most distant realms; it is by devoting myself to extensive botanical study, by examining nature unremittingly, observing both its constancy and variety of shapes and colours, that I believe finally to have succeeded, by the triple means of exactitude, composition and colouring, the union of which only, may bring to perfection the iconography of plants.[2]

The original works were reproduced by stipple engraving, which was said to be particularly suited to the reproduction of botanical detail. Redouté famously had as his pupils or patrons five queens and empresses of France, from Marie-Antoinette to Empress Marie-Louise of Austria. As the established 'Draughtsman and Painter to the Queen's Cabinet', his position was a difficult one during the Revolution but his skill with the brush enabled him to move almost seamlessly on, via a spell at the Royal Botanic Gardens at Kew (London), to recording the flower collections of Empress Joséphine at Malmaison. Although roses and lilies were always his favourites, and those of his aristocratic patrons and pupils, the inclusion in the *Choix des belles fleurs* of what he knew as the *oeillet panache* betrays his love of the flower. A further posy of four carnations in 'self' colours of deep red, purple, white and yellow entitled *Oeillet varieté*, indicates the range of carnation colours available to his patrons in early nineteenth-century France.

Despite having a markedly different style, Pierre-Joseph Redouté was often hailed as the successor to the still-life artists of the seventeenth- and eighteenth-century Low Countries. Known as the 'Golden Age' artists, their still-lifes often included the new 'florists flowers' of the period (most usually the unpredictable tulip), or favoured the religious symbolism of the iris or the rosemary sprig. The adaptable carnation slipped easily into both categories and can be seen in all its striped glory in paintings such as Balthasar van der Ast's *Still-life of a Semper Augustus Tulip, Irises, a Carnation and Other Flowers in a Wan-Li Vase*. The carnation was in expensive company as the 'Semper Augustus' tulip was priced at 1,000 Dutch guilders in the 1620s, rising to over 5,000 guilders just before the 'crash' of 'Tulipmania' in the late 1630s. The carnation never reached such heights but the same 'flamed' and striped forms appear in the paintings of the period. Balthasar van der Ast (1593/4–1657) was one of the Dutch 'Golden Age' painters and most of his works feature a variety of flowers with a scattering of shells, lizards and fruits, but one unusual work focuses almost solely on carnations. *Floral Study: Carnations in a Vase* depicts six carnations in various forms, including striped and selfs in shades of palest pink to bold red, set against a black background. Now housed in the Leeds Art Gallery, the detailing of the individual petals with their varying degrees of serration or 'pinking', the slight spotting on the central flower and the bold stripes of the topmost, look as exquisite today as they must have done when they were painted almost four hundred years ago.

These 'Golden Age' paintings with their collection of flowers frequently depict carnations sharing a basket or vase with flowers and fruits of all seasons: roses, peonies, marigolds, ripe cherries, apricots and even pomegranates appear together in an era long before the 'perpetual' carnation. The van der Ast painting of carnations envisages them sharing the vase with fritillary, crocus and cyclamen, as well as a precocious rose, while Jan Davidsz. de Heem (1606–1684) portrayed his carnations next to bursting ripe figs, blushing grapes, peaches and springtime tulips. Rather than the product of a forcing house or glasshouse, the paintings were often created by a skilful addition of each plant through the seasons. More realistic at least in their groupings were the themed 'monthly' paintings that became popular in the early eighteenth century, promoted by artists and nurserymen alike. Typically shown in vases depicting the signs of the zodiac or mythical deities appropriate to the month, these could be boastful or optimistic, but they at least had a basis in

This botanical illustration from the 17th-century Gottorfer Codex takes on the quality of modern poster art.

the reality of what might be in a wealthy person's garden in the appropriate month. Carnations figured in the months from June to October in the *Twelve Months of Flowers* published in 1730 by the Kensington nurseryman Robert Furber, but were realistically lacking through the winter months and early spring. Furber was able to gain 450 subscribers to his 'catalogue' plates and presumably gained even more from the sale of the plants that these advertised, with one set of plates for flowers and another for fruits. The listings below the images were designed to tempt wealthy clients into ordering by number in what is thought to be the earliest garden catalogue in the world.

After the impossible pyramids of flowers that burst forth from the small vases of Furber's *Twelve Months of Flowers*, it is a relief to turn to the more strictly botanical works, where only the range of colours and patterns give rise to envy in the heart of the gardener. Created for the physician and botanist Robert Thornton, the illustrations for his *Temple of Flora* included some of the most expensive botanical depictions of the carnation ever produced. Thornton was inspired by the work of the Swedish botanist and zoologist Carl Linnaeus (1707–1778), who established the 'modern' system of the naming of all living organisms with two Latin names, as well as establishing

A striped carnation flaunts itself alongside the striped tulip in
Jan Davidsz. de Heem's *Memento Mori*, c. 1665, oil on canvas.

their relationships and their sexuality. In the 1790s Thornton ambitiously embarked on an illustrated guide to Linnaeus's system, including as Part (Volume) III a 'Temple of Flora', with seventy full-sized folio plates, newly illustrated by Philip Reinagle and Peter Charles Henderson and then engraved in aquatint, stipple and line by engravers including Thomas Medland and Joseph Constantine. The cost of the project for this volume alone was outrageous.

Group of carnations, engraved by Maddox after a painting by Peter Henderson, from Dr Robert Thornton's *The Temple of Flora* (c. 1807).

Thornton hastily included a page dedicating the work to the foremost patron of botany and art of the period, Queen Charlotte of Mecklenburg-Strelitz, wife of George III and herself a collector of picotees. However, royal finance failed to appear and, despite inheriting the family fortune on the death of his brother, Thornton was forced to hold a public lottery to try and stave off his losses. Only 33 of the illustrations were eventually created, including the life-sized carnations. Thornton never really recovered from the loss and despite publishing a work on *The British Flora* in 1812, he died destitute thirty years after the carnations had appeared. The carnations meanwhile took on an artistic life of their own, appearing as individual prints in drawing rooms across the country. They can still be found, as prints for sale, slightly altered or placed against a different backdrop and claiming to be a different work altogether. In the original by Henderson, six carnations and a bud portrayed the range of flakes and fancies, laced in pink, red and a purple just a step away from blue. The backdrop, as with all the plates in the *Temple of Flora*, was a vaguely exotic scene of lakes and hills with a building to the right that might be an orangery or hothouse. What was more surprising was the company the carnations kept within the book. The plates that were eventually created included the 'Quadrangular Passion Flower', the 'Dragon Arum', 'American Bog Plants', 'the Aloe' and the mysterious 'Night Blowing Circus'. Only the tulip (suitably flamed), the auricula and the snowdrop would have seemed familiar to the English gardeners as suitable companions for the carnation.

Thornton had as his inspiration the numerous books of flora that had preceded him and had quietly replaced the earlier 'herbals'. Many of these had used the flower collections of their patrons as the basis of their works: Pierre Vallet's *Le Jardin de roy très chrestien, Louis XIII, roy de France* of 1623, or the painter Nicolas Robert's portrayals of the Duke of Orléans's collection in the mid-seventeenth century. However, many later artists drew inspiration from their own gardens, albeit on a smaller scale. From 1876 onwards the French artist Ignace

Édouard Manet, *Carnations and Clematis in a Crystal Vase*, c. 1882, oil on canvas.

Henri Théodore Fantin-Latour concentrated his work on the contents of the gardens at Buré in France, inherited by his wife from her uncle. Here Henri and his wife Victoria Dubourg, herself a successful artist, planted flowers specifically to provide material for their paintings, including the long-lasting carnations and delicate pinks whose scents sadly did not transfer to the canvases. Introduced to the English market by his friend Whistler, Fantin-Latour's flower paintings sold so well in London through patrons such as Edwin and Ruth Edwards that it was said they were practically unknown in France during his lifetime. The carnations he depicted were predominantly 'selfs', of one colour, with large multi-petalled blooms. In one a glass full of pure white carnations against a dark background stands out as though freshly picked and carelessly placed in the first receptacle that came to hand, their stems just fitting into the space available. Another depicts a mix of pinks, purples and whites in a champagne glass. Mixed with roses and peonies, they reveal the riches of the garden at Buré. The money Fantin-Latour received for his still-lifes allowed him to indulge his portraiture, including group portraits with his close friends and fellow artists such as Delacroix and Édouard Manet (1832–1883), who also included flower still-lifes within his own *oeuvre*, although in a markedly more modern style than his friend. Manet's *Carnations and Clematis in a Crystal Vase* (c. 1882) shows, rather than the bunched and heavily petalled carnations of Fantin-Latour's garden, a slim and merely doubled pale pink flower that more closely resembles a simple pink, upstaged by the single showy purple/blue clematis flower.

However entrancing as floral specimens, portrayals of the carnation take on an additional interest when they form just part of an image that seems to have a wider story. In some instances these are easily 'decoded' using the symbolism of carnations in religion, or the association between the carnation and love, betrothal and wedlock, as explored in earlier chapters. The Hampden Portrait of Elizabeth I, for example, portrays her clasping a carnation as a symbol of her betrothal to God and her country. Elizabeth's mother Anne Boleyn

A modern
photograph
echoes Manet's
carnations.

also clasps a red carnation in a more sombre portrait of thirty years earlier, denoting her (ill-fated) marriage to Henry VIII. The self-portrait of the artist Otto Dix (1891–1969) similarly uses a carnation to refer back to a previous painting, in this case identifying himself with artists of the fifteenth and sixteenth centuries who did the same. Other paintings are more complex or downright intriguing. In 1925 the Swiss artist Félix Edouard Vallotton (1865–1925) chose a stone-ware vase of deep red carnations to place on his table next to his account books in a painting entitled simply *Oeillets et livre de comptes*. A red-handled pen balanced on an inkpot takes up the colour. Vallotton appears to have been fascinated by oranges and reds in these last years of his life, depicting various vases of nasturtiums and baskets of bright cherries. In 1910 a critic had said of Vallotton that the colours in his paintings 'lack all joyfulness', but the vases of tulips and carnations from the 1920s have a life force that reaches its peak in *Oeillets et livre de comptes*, perhaps denoting a defiance against the accounts of a life without wealth, and the cancer that was soon to end it. Equally intriguing is the painting *The Suffragette's House* by Tirzah Ravilious (née Garwood), wife of the watercolour painter and printer Eric Ravilious. A blue 'doll's house' nestles on a lawn surrounded by tiny peg-like dolls dressed in carnation petal skirts, each appearing to whirl like dervishes in a dance. All except one wear a 'laced' pink with a yellow centre, the other being a striking poppy coloured with sateen black eye. Watching over the scene, as tall as a tree reaching the roof of the diminutive house, is a heavily fringed pure white dianthus with its petals so cut and indented as to form a lacework in contrast to the heavy skirts of the dancers. The image is probably an accidental modern version of Francis Bacon's famous *Masque of Flowers* on the occasion of the marriage between the Earl and Countess of Somerset, when tulips and 'pots of Gilliflowers' came alive on the stage.

Anita Magsaysay-Ho, *Women with Carnations*, 1990, oil on canvas.

Art Nouveau poster,
'The Flowers:
Carnation', by
Alphonse Mucha,
1898.

Dancers also appear, rather differently clothed, in Botticelli's glorious painting entitled *La primavera*, perhaps the most famous of paintings originally commissioned by the great fifteenth-century gardening family, the Medicis of Florence. The 'Three Graces' are the dancers, but it is Flora (or Primavera) who catches our attention in a dress covered with embroidered plants. Botticelli would have been able to draw on the wealth of rare and beautiful plants in the gardens of the Medici villas, such as the Villa Castello where the painting originally hung, but most of the two hundred plants that have been identified are those of the meadows and simpler gardens of Renaissance Italy. Among those in the meadow are wild pinks, while on her dress Flora has embroidered carnations and pinks in the style of the botanic books of the period: a coming together between divine myth, botany, art and needlework courtesy of the carnation and the Medici.

eight

A Strengthener of the Heart and Brain

Jove was my sire, to me he did impart
(Who best deserv'd) the Empire of the heart,
Let him with golden Aspect please the Eye,
A sov'reign cordial to the heart am I,
Not Tagus nor the Treasury of Peru,
Thy boasted soil can grief, like me subdue.
Should Jove once more descend in golden show'r,
Not Jove could prove so cordial as my flower.

. . .

Most lib'rally my Bounty I impart,
'Tis Joy to mine to ease another's Heart.
Some flowers for physick serve, and some for smell,
For beauty some – but I in all excell.
ABRAHAM COWLEY, 'July-flower',
in *Six Books of Plants* (1668)

'Consumption, constipation, pestilence and poison', a collection of ills for which no one flower might be thought to have power enough to act against, are nevertheless all conditions for which the carnation has been recommended. The enthusiastic carnation lover the Baron de Ponsort even claimed that it had been used to bring men back from the dead.[1] In the Renaissance period in Europe, white wine was infused with the petals (which were steeped until they were pale and then strained out) and was drunk as a nerve tonic 'to help those whose constitution is inclinable to be consumptive. It is good to expel poison and help hot pestilent fevers.' The German herbalist Leonhart Fuchs (1501–1566) believed that the root was useful against the plague, while the juice could dissolve kidney and bladder stones, a property of enormous value in an era before anaesthetic when operations for 'the stone' could leave you dead from pain or shock – if 'blockage of the stone' had not already killed you. The plague referred to by Fuchs was the bubonic plague, prevalent in Europe at this time, against which no flower could hope to battle, but perhaps a general comfort might be obtained even if a cure was not, as he explains in his work *De historia stirpium commentarii insignes* (Notable Commentaries on the History of Plants), originally published in 1542: 'they [carnations] are great strengtheners of the brain and heart, and will therefore make an excellent cordial for family purposes. Either the conserve or syrup of these flowers taken at intervals, is good.' The French writer A. Karr went further in his *Voyage autour de mon jardin*, declaring not only that 'the distilled water of gillyflowers is an excellent remedy for the falling sickness' but that 'if one makes a conserve of

Dried carnations and roses along with other herbs.

it it is the life and delight of the human race'.[2] The apothecary John Gerard, writing his *Herball, or General Historie of Plants* in 1597, noted that 'A water distilled from Pinks has been commended as excellent for curing epilepsy,' and 'a conserve made of the flowers with sugar is exceeding cordial, and wonderfully above measure doth comfort the heart, being eaten now and then', adding that it was the life and delight of the human race. It is as a comfort and joy to the heart, as Abraham Cowley says, that he promoted the primacy of the carnation above the tulip and the 'emony' (anemone) in his 1668 *Six Books of Plants*, a multi-volume collection of his works.

Just forty years earlier, in 1629, John Parkinson was already overwhelmed by the sheer variety of carnations and pinks by then available, and gave most of his attention in his *Paradisi in sole, paradisus terrestris* to describing the colours and types of flower from white to orange to tawny, from flaked to striped to speckled, but ended by concluding that it was

> The red or Clove Gilleflower that is most used in Physicke in our Apothecaries shops, none of the other being accepted of or used (and yet I doubt not, but all of them might serve, and to good purpose although not to give so gallant a tincture to a Syrupe as the ordinary red will doe) and is accounted to be very Cordiall.

What exactly it was 'cordiall' for he did not reveal, and an all-round tonic or comforter may perhaps be read into the term in keeping with Gerard and Cowley's claims. The comforting quality of the carnation was estimated to be less present in the pink, despite its scent, and Gerard, in his *Herball*, dismisses the pink as having 'small effect' as 'It is thought by diverse, that their virtues are answerable to the Gilleflowers, yet . . . they are little use with us'. The larger, closely related sweet william suffered even greater ignominy, being dismissed by Parkinson as not known ever to have been used in physicke – a statement rarely seen in books prior to the seventeenth century when it was thought that all flowers and plants had a use, or else why would God have created them? Parkinson's was one of the first treatises to celebrate flowers for their beauty rather than their use, but for many years this stance would remain almost heretical. In the mid-seventeenth century the astrological herbalist Nicholas Culpeper, taking his lead from Fuchs in the previous century, noted that 'Carnations . . . are great strengtheners both of heart and brain' and this combination of body and soul would have conveniently fortified you against some of the worst dangers of contemporary society, as noted in his *The English Physician* (1652): 'Three kinds of people mainly disease the people – priests, physicians and lawyers – priests disease matters belonging to their souls, physicians disease matters belonging to their bodies, and lawyers disease matters belonging to their estate.' More prosaically, should you be of sound heart and mind and not bothered with plague, stone or epilepsy, the petals could be steeped in rosewater and used as hair perfume through the Tudor and Elizabethan period, while the French physician and botanist Jean Ruel (1474–1537) recommended placing the flower in vinegar to impart a 'pleasant taste and gallant colour' – presumably to the vinegar rather than the flower.

The strong scent of the carnation led to its use by the French philosopher René Descartes as an illustration of his famous theory of the nature of interaction between the mind and the body. Descartes (1596–1650), most famous for his statement *cogito ergo sum* (I think therefore I am), struggled to explain the mechanistic determination of reflex or causal relations. He hypothesized that the mind interacted with the body at the pineal gland, which he felt formed the seat of the soul, and sensations experienced by the body, such as the inhalation of the heady perfume of the dianthus, made their way to the gland, causing it to vibrate and in turn give rise to emotions. This dualistic explanation could also be used to explain the healing and comforting process provided by the body for the mind – especially useful after a long day of contemplating whether doubting doubt actually proves existence. In a set of engravings of 'The Five Senses' illustrating Descartes' theories for the more simple-minded reader, a gardener stoops to pick a carnation. Instinctively lifting it to his nose in anticipation, he inhales its scent and half drops his working spade, perhaps infused with the comfort that Gerard predicted.

Gardeners had long realized the calming effect of weeding the carnation bed, and as early as 1618 William Lawson declared in his *Country Housewife's Garden* that the carnation's use was 'much in ornament, and comforting the spirits by the sense of smelling'. At a simpler level, comfort and invigoration were also looked for with success by the amateur 'florist' and nurseryman Thomas Hogg. When Hogg published his second edition of *Florists' Flowers* in 1822, he was already a celebrated florist specializing in the pink (naming 154 varieties), but he stated, 'I am neither gardener nor florist professionally, but that I commenced the cultivation of flowers, in the first instance, with a view to amuse a depressed state of mind, and reinvigorate a still more sickly state of body.' His success in these aims may be judged

The poetic feelings of the poet were associated with pinks and carnations, as depicted on this French vintage plate.

Gardener smelling a carnation or pink, used in depiction of his 'senses', in the 17th century. Engraving after set of 'The Five Senses' by David Teniers the Younger.

by the fine blooms he produced and the excellent papers he wrote on his favourite flowers, banishing his depression and staying well away from Cartesian philosophy!

Scented pinks also appear in a booklet produced several centuries ahead of its time by the diarist and gardener John Evelyn. In his gloriously spelt *Fumifugium: or The Inconveniencie of the Aer and Smoak of London Disspiated* (1661), Evelyn proposed a scheme whereby London would be surrounded by garden plots, each of some 30 or 40 acres and each containing sweetly odiferous plants, leaves and flowers, so that the air of London might be sweetened and purified. This was a vital consideration in a period when the bad odours and miasmas of the London air were thought to harbour the source of a wide range of diseases, including the plague that had so recently devastated the city. Smoke

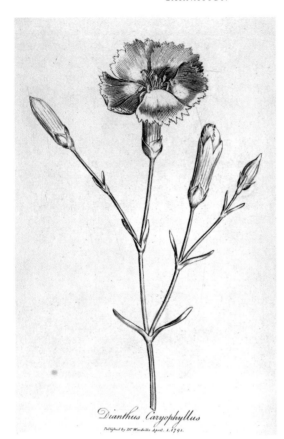

Dianthus caryophyllus
from a Woodville
book on medical
botany (1792).

Dianthus Caryophyllus
Published by Dr Woodville April 1. 1791.

too was disturbing the city and its inhabitants, argued Evelyn, and
the only prevention lay in an act to limit the burning of coals, combined with the creation of sweet-smelling open spaces. Among the
syringa, rosemary, lavender, rose, honeysuckle and juniper that were
to form the shrubs within these gardens and 'tinge the Air upon
every gentle emission at a great distance' were to be 'beds and borders
of pinks, carnations, clove, stock-gilly-flower, primroses, auriculas and
violets, not forgetting the white', alongside other herbs which 'upon
the least pressure and cutting breathe out and betray their ravishing
odours'.

Toiletries of the late nineteenth and twentieth centuries looked
back to these pre-industrial eras and included sweet clove scent in

a range of women's scents and soaps. In the 1940s the company Luxor made 'Carnation' soaps and hand lotions while the rather more upmarket Bouquet Lentheric au Parfum Carnation was most popular between the wars, Bouquet Lentheric was advertised in the late 1930s against a sophisticated dark background with just a hint of Art Deco. While Bouquet Lentheric was advertised as 'the daytime fragrance', the heavier Oeillet Bleu by Roger & Gallet was famously associated with women who had confidence in their own sensuality and were happy to broadcast this. Other classic perfumes with a carnation-based scent included Caron Fleurs de Rocaille (still available over eighty years since its launch in 1934) and Floris Malmaison. For those who preferred a more subtle carnation scent, various eaux de toilettes and soaps were available, and even carnation talcum powder. The English company J. P. Williams specialized in floral talcum powders and cold creams at the start of the twentieth century and released highly decorated tins redolent of the period. The modern carnation lover can purchase Comme des Garçons Series 2: Red Carnation, which is said (by the producers) to harbour basenotes of red pepper, red rose, cloves and Egyptian jasmine, as well as velvety carnation. It

Ideally suited for all gardeners and planters, *Dianthus*
can waft its comforting scent in all situations.

comes in a bright red bottle whose vibrant hue would delight the heart of carnation breeders everywhere. The compound eugenol is what gives the carnation its sweet, heavy scent, most often copied by modern producers of cheaper scents than those by Comme de Garçons, and perfume producers who desire a hint of carnation at less expense will use a combination of clove, black pepper and ylang ylang.

Also making use of the bright red carnation until recently was the well-known brand Carnation Corn Caps – soft felt rings used to comfort and medicate hard patches on the feet which were so common in the past with tight or ill-fitting hard leather shoes. The carnation was a trademark and had nothing to do with the contents of the patch, which was impregnated with salicylic acid to help soften hard skin. Until recently salicylic acid had no other connection to carnation flowers other than the branding for a foot product, but recent experiments have proved that adding a small amount of acid to a vase of water helps prolong the life of cut flowers, and for their experiments scientists used carnations.

Many of the early recipes for using carnations and pinks as a 'medicine' refer not to the inhalation of scents but to the ingestion of the flowers. These were also regarded as a delicacy as well as a curative. In the Middle Ages, the petals were used as a substitute for cloves, which were more expensive and had to be imported. In Elizabethan times the highly fragrant flowers were steeped in wine

Carnation Corn Caps ironically contain no carnation.

and ale to make a delightful drink. 'Sops', small pieces of toast or stale bread, were offered as solid food for dipping in the tasty liquid, or 'soppes-in-wine'. In her garden of edible plants at the Manor House in Stevington in Bedfordshire, Kathy Brown grows the highly scented old-fashioned pinks, including 'Mrs Sinkins' and 'Doris', and the tiny dwarf Alpines such as 'Whatfield Can-can' and 'Betty Norton' for flavouring sugars, oils and vinegars. The company Suttons Seeds encourages gardeners to grow its 'Giant Chabaud' mix of carnations to add petals to salads. Although dating back only to the nineteenth century rather than the Tudor period, crystallized petals decorate cakes and meringues and complement almond biscuits. For all edible uses the petal must be detached carefully from the flower head and the white 'heel' at the base of the petal removed, as its bitter taste would totally spoil the delicate hint of spicy scented clove.

For those hoping to taste exotically coloured carnations, the Blue Carnation cocktail might seem an excellent starting point. A cocktail guide describes it as a beautiful pale colour, perfect for showers, receptions and spring affairs. However, disappointment awaits the true carnation enthusiast as it contains no carnation at all, being created of white crème de cacao, blue curaçao and cream. Perhaps one could add a carnation petal to float on the top to keep the promise of its name.

Surprisingly, the delicate edibility of the carnation had nothing to do with the naming of the now famous Carnation Evaporated Milk. Founded in 1899 by Eldridge Amos Stuart (1856–1944) as the Pacific Coast Condensed Milk Company, the aim was to provide a safe and sterile dairy product in the days before refrigeration. In 1901 Stuart was casting around for a new name for the company and happened to notice a display of cigars in a tobacconist's shop with the name 'Carnation'. The adoption of the carnation allowed Stuart to develop his famous, alliterative advertising slogan 'Carnation Condensed Milk, Milk from Contented Cows'. Through the 1930s and '40s, when fresh milk became scarce in some countries during the war, advertisements for Carnation Milk emphasized the role it

WILL'S CIGARETTES

ANNUAL CARNATION
Variety : GIANT CHABAUD MIXED

'Chabaud' can be grown for eating as well as admiring.

could play in keeping children and mothers healthy and full of vitality. Full-page advertisements in American and English periodicals such as *Woman's Own* were devoted to images of homecoming fathers delighted with blancmanges and other milky puddings made of the vaguely sweet-tasting milk. The Carnation Company was taken over by Nestlé in 1985, but retained the original name and the attractive posy of red and white carnations on the can, complete with suggested recipes. The mystery remains, however, of why the cigar that inspired the choice was called 'Carnation' in the first place.

Traditional Chinese medicine also gives a prominent role to the carnation, using both *Dianthus superbus* and – appropriately – *Dianthus chinensis* (or *sinensis*). To create the medicinal herb Qu Mai from the Dianthus, the stems as well as the flowers are utilized. Qu Mai is used to promote uterine contractions and acts as a short-term diuretic, as well as being used for 'heat strangury', boils and carbuncles, bringing a positively seventeenth-century flavour to the list of ills it can help with. Its role in uterine contractions makes it a dangerous drug for pregnant women, who should avoid ingesting it either raw or dried, but it is said to be harmless when its scent is inhaled to gain comfort. The *Dianthus chinensis* in particular is described in Chinese medicine as having a 'bitter, cold' humour, and is thus traditionally associated with the bladder, small intestine and heart. Recent unsubstantiated claims have also been made for a role in the treatment of oesophageal

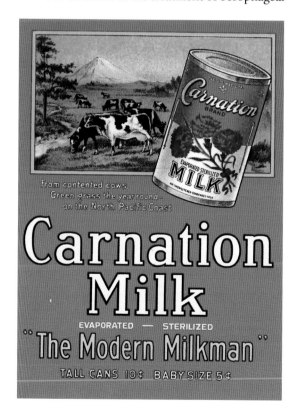

Carnation Milk offered a healthy and safe option for dairy consumption in a world before refridgerators.

石竹花

カ ラ ナ デ シ コ

花弁 表ヌンジ具金画。裏全淡住王

葉 表白三緑、裏白緑

蕾芭茎比白緑ヌンジ曲

裏白緑山曲中ニシベ

Karanadeshiko,
sekichiku or China
pink. Handcoloured
woodblock print
by Kono Bairei from
Senshu No Hana (One
Thousand Kinds
of Flowers, 1891).

and colon cancer. Growing and harvesting traditionally takes place
in China in the areas of Hebei, Henan, Liaoning and Jiangsu, where
it is usually harvested in summer and autumn during flowering and
fruiting time, after which the flowers, leaves and stalks are dried
in the sun before being cut up into small pieces for later making
into powder, adding to decoctions or eating. As with all traditional
medicines, debate continues on the manner in which the plants work
and which of their chemical constituents might, or might not, be
effective. Carnation tea was also very popular in ancient China for

its ability to relax the spirit and promote energy and vitality. The teas often included all of the carnation plant, from its flowers to its petals and roots, and were used to reduce muscle tension.

An association with drugs, although in this instance not medicinal, still impacts on the largest producers of carnations in the twenty-first century. Colombia, renowned in the 1980s for its supply of cocaine into North America, used its flower industry to disguise the drugs, which were hidden among crates of roses and carnations. The overwhelming scent of the flowers stymied attempts by sniffer dogs to locate the illicit drugs as they passed through border controls. Drug traffickers paid flower producers handsomely for 'piggy backing' on their trade and the growers were in effect a subsidized industry. An unintended consequence was the sudden growth (in all senses) of the Colombian flower-growing industry. Flourishing on the high sunny plateaus outside Colombia's two largest cities, Bogotá and Medellín, the flower fields provided work for tens of thousands of female labourers, many of whom would otherwise have struggled to feed their families. In 1994 Colombia supplied one-tenth of the world's flower exports, 60 per cent of all flowers sold in the U.S. and 97 per cent of carnations. Roses, the second favourite of the Colombian growers, were said to be worth U.S. $100 million a year and 50,000 jobs. This supply, which was said to threaten the livelihood of U.S. flower growers, ironically also provided income and jobs for the areas around Miami International Airport where climate-control facilities had to be specifically constructed to cope with the flower imports, and in 1992 Orlando Airport followed suit in a bid to gain more of the lucrative trade. By 2003 the United States imported 2 billion major blooms a year and grew only 200 million – although increased industrialization and regulation means that it is unlikely that a bunch of flowers purchased for Mother's Day will any longer contain a surprising and stimulating addition in the form of a packet of cocaine!

A final reference to the health-inducing qualities of the dianthus might be thought to appear in the phrase 'in the pink', used as an affirmation of being in the best of health and spirits. The origins of this simple declaration are, however, more complex than might be expected. Many presume it to be a reference to the possession of healthy pink cheeks, deriving themselves from the naming of the colour 'pink' from the flower, although ironically the term 'carnation', rather than pink, was used in the seventeenth century to describe the pink-coloured blush on ripe fruits and maidenly cheeks. Others suggest that the phrase is related to the wearing of 'hunting pink', the distinctive red or scarlet jacket of the foxhunter. However, more detailed research indicates an older derivation to be from the term 'at the "pinke", or, in modern phraseology, 'at the pinnacle'. In Shakespeare's *Romeo and Juliet* (1597), Mercutio declares that he is 'the very pinke of courtesie', and by the early eighteenth century in the rather appropriately entitled play *Kensington Gardens*, the playwright and actor John Leigh declared in character that ''Tis the Pink of the Mode, to marry at first Sight: And some, indeed, marry without any Sight at all.' In fact John Leigh (*c.* 1689–1726?), nicknamed 'handsome Leigh', was not of the marrying kind, as the later phrase would have it. A contemporary, W. R. Chetwood, declared in his *A General History of the Stage* (1749) that he 'might have been in the good Graces of the Fair-Sex, if his taste had led him that way', and one wonders if, had he been alive two hundred years later, he might have boasted instead the green carnation beloved of Oscar Wilde. By the nineteenth century 'in the pink' was commonly used to express extremes of either the peak of attainment or the depths. In 1845 Charles Dickens wrote in a letter: 'Of all the picturesque abominations in the World, commend me to Fondi. It is the very pink of hideousness and squalid misery' – a statement that places a libellous injustice on both the Italian town of Fondi and the heart-warming dianthus which had steadfastly acted as a tonic against such human misery.

Modern practitioners of essential oils have given the gentle phrasing of the old herbal a modern makeover and now the *Dianthus caryophyllus* is described as alexiteric, antispasmodic, cardiotonic, diaphoretic and nervine, which means much the same as the Elizabethan

A FIELD OF CARNATIONS

Prior to the rise of the South American market, the southern USA
grew extensive fields of carnations.

prescription for comfort and uplifting, but rephrased for a world
obsessed with science. It is the heady scent of the oils that is usually
used to promote healing through aromatherapy rather than ingestion,
and this harks back to centuries of use. Carnation oil is also popular
applied externally, again because it helps promote relaxation, but it is
also claimed to promote skin regeneration, make skin softer and leave
a sweet and soothing scent. It is additionally used to treat skin irrita-
tion and rashes. Many commercial growers of modern essential oils
are based in France, famed for its traditional use of herbs and flowers.
It takes 500 kg of flower heads to produce 100 g of oil, with flowers
ideally harvested just three hours after opening to the morning sun-
light, although synthetics of eugenol, isoeugenol and eugenyl acetate
are also used. Yellow and orange varieties do not carry any scent and
so the trade is confined to the traditional pink pinks and the clove
carnation, reminding us of Parkinson's comments on the use of these
same colours almost four hundred years ago. For those not patient
enough to grow and press 500 kg of flower heads, individual flowers
can also be used in potpourri, or substituted for roses in syrups and
candied petals.

'The Pink of Politeness and a Prim Rose', 1821, satirical print.

Before leaving the peaceful spiritual uses of the carnation, a final note on those who wage war on its health-giving growth. Rabbits and hares (the latter sadly an unlikely visitor to the garden in modern times) are said to favour the dianthus above all other contents of the cottage flower garden for their crepuscular feeds. In 1840 Louisa Johnson (*Every Lady Her own Flower Gardener*) recommended that pots of pinks be placed on raised platforms to keep them away from prospective nibblers, while other writers suggest that spreading straw around plants or crisscrossing the area with raised thread will be sufficient to put off rabbits, both proposals that seem extremely unlikely to work unless the rabbit is already replete. After the rabbit and hare, the earwig is said to do the most damage to the dianthus, although rarely eating the entire plant from root upwards. Instead, the damage is to the flower head so prized of florists. Thomas Hogg recommended placing pots of prized plants on stools with each leg of the stool in water to prevent earwigs arriving at the plant at all, a sort of miniature moated defence. For those that made it through this barricade, a 'decoy' should be set up around the carnation in the form of upside-down pots or cones containing straw or other cosy material. Here the earwigs and other insects would find a second home, only to be rudely awakened (briefly) when the pot was emptied out and its residents shaken into water. It seems a cruel procedure but at least they would have died in the happiest content-ment, strengthened in heart and brain by the scent wafting through their temporary home.

nine

Crossing Continents: The Tangled Web of the Perpetual Carnation

꿍

Here Spring perpetual leads the laughing hours,

And Winter wears a wreath of Summer flowers

SOTHEBY'S VIRGIL, quoted in William Curtis's *Botanical Magazine*, 1827

The time is early nineteenth-century Europe, the scene a small nursery in Lyons, France; the characters a French gardener, a Chinese carnation (*Dianthus chinensis* or *sinensis*) and the original *Dianthus caryophyllus*. The storyline is the creation of the first ever 'perpetual' flowering carnation, flowering repeatedly ('remontant') through the winter with bigger and better blooms than either of its parents. But first there is the prelude. In 1750 in the commune of Ollioules at the extreme south of France, a 'carnation Mayonnais' named 'Oeillet De Mahon' was coaxed into flowering continuously from late spring through to September, but further into the autumn it would not venture. There matters rested for almost eighty years until that fateful day when, at the nurseries of Monsieur Laceme of Lyons (a city that used to be a centre of horti-culture), a gardener named Dalmais crossed a variety of the 'Oeillet De Mahon' with an 'Oeillet Bisbon' to produce a striped carna-tion that flowered repeatedly through the long summer and into the autumn. Further crossings with varieties including 'Grenadon' and 'St Antoine', all favourites of the French nurseries, resulted in a wealth of solid pink and red flowers, *et voilà!* – the longed-for French remontant carnation was born.

NEW YELLOW PERPETUAL CARNATION
QUEEN OF SPAIN.

Perpetual carnation 'Queen of Spain', a popular perpetual in the Edwardian period.

However, as is the way with florists and nurserymen, having achieved their heart's desire, what was there left to do but improve it? A fellow Lyons nurseryman took up the baton and a Monsieur Schmidt (or possibly Scmitt) devoted years to developing a wider range of colours, including varieties such as 'Arc-En-Ciel' (rainbow) and 'Étoile Polaire', before disease destroyed his entire collection in 1850. Ironically, weakness to such a fate was most likely to have been introduced by M. Schmidt himself through too much interbreeding and the creation of over-rich soils in his desperation to produce

WILLS'S CIGARETTES.

CARNATION.

This cigarette card
of the perpetual
carnation has an
Art Nouveau quality.

the perfect specimen. Schmidt fell by the wayside, heartbroken at
his losses, but there was no shortage of Lyonnais nurserymen to
follow in his footsteps. In 1866 Alphonse Alegatière used propaga-
tion through layering rather than cuttings to further what has been
described as the greatest of all horticultural dreams, boldly declaring
that the hunt for the *truly* perpetual carnation was over.

Having already been responsible for that most magnificent of
flowers, the Malmaison carnation, the French had now created a

dianthus that would greet you with enthusiasm throughout the year – or at least, if they were totally honest, most of the year. Of course it helped if you lived in the south of France with a long warm summer to help build up the plant's reserves, and a mild autumn and winter to fool it into flowering. Even then, in order to achieve 'perpetual' flowering, not only did the correct plant have to be obtained but the correct horticultural technique had to be applied. The new remontant carnations had to be closely managed by the shortening back in spring and early summer of all the taller or elongated shoots that had formed so that a fresh growth could be induced at that period; these would then develop through the late summer to produce a succession of flowers through the autumn and into winter. They also needed lots of room to stretch their roots and constant attention to the temperature and moisture so that they did not suffer checks or setbacks. They were on the whole a fussy lot. However, the diligent nurserymen of Lyons did not flag, and by the 1880s commercial success was well on its way.

Decades had now passed since the diligent gardener Dalmais had produced the first (almost) remontant, and in England and America competition was brewing. Whether there had been an independent discovery, or whether the Lyons nurserymen had been foolish enough to let some of their creations slip through their hands, a crimson-flowered carnation that flowered into the winter had been spotted in England at almost the same time as those in France. In December 1861 *The Gardeners' Chronicle* recalled that 'Some forty years ago it seems, the first variety of tree carnations, one with crimson flowers, made its way into our gardens.' If the writer in *The Gardeners' Chronicle* was correct (and in this august periodical aimed at the professional gardener they usually were), then the tree carnation must have first appeared in England almost simultaneously with its creation in France. The article goes on to explain that these first arrivals, owing their origins to 'the intelligent skill of some far-seeing florist', had strangely been lost (perhaps indicative of a few solitary imports from France) and that further imports from Belgian florists had similarly failed. The tide had turned in 1860 when the Royal Horticultural Society had recognized their existence with an Award of Special Merit, and by 1861 there were some eighty cultivars known in England. The value of these 'perpetual flowering' or 'tree' carnations, according to *The Gardeners' Chronicle*, was predominantly in their use for indoor decoration in pots, and for winter bouquets 'of the higher class'.

From this first recognition in the mid-nineteenth century, well into the twentieth, these 'perpetually' flowering plants were indeed to be the privilege of the wealthy and dedicated. In addition to the prohibitive cost of obtaining a large quantity of plants suitable for making a 'show', one had to obtain a commensurate large quantity of gardeners to tend them. The 'principal' or main horticultural techniques needing to be applied to ensure happily flowering plants included, according to *The Gardeners' Chronicle*: at the end of the previous season cutting away all the old stems immediately after flowering and placing the plants in a dry cool pit (such as a small glass-covered protective construction) then keeping the plants well ventilated and freely exposed to light but protected from frost; as they started to expand in the spring, re-potting and top-dressing; in late spring when the danger of frosts was passed, planting them out in summer quarters in ready prepared beds on a dry subsoil with a foot and a half of pulverized fertile soil enriched with leaf mould and cow manure in a light and dry situation; in case of a late frost or heavy rain a portable glass frame should be at hand to cover them with. Immediately after any such rain the soil around them should be 'stirred' to re-open it and encourage drainage.

Come September the plants could be re-lifted from their summer quarters into pots and kept two to three weeks in a greenhouse or pit again with some shade or protection being provided at the heat of the day. Watering should be carried out in small amounts but with constant attention.

As the season progressed the occasional outing to a warmer greenhouse at 50–60 degrees Fahrenheit was recommended, as the anxious gardener inspected them for swelling flower buds.

By late autumn/early winter the plants could be divided between those that were responding to this elaborate garden ritual by coming into flower, and those that sadly would need another full year of this peripatetic lifestyle before favouring their owners with a display of flowers.

Finally in early to mid-winter the anxious gardener and his visitors would be rewarded by a show of flowers which, with further

This catalogue of the Boston-based seed merchant Rawson's dates to the period when perpetuals were becoming most popular.

careful and ongoing management and pinching out of shoots and buds, would bloom through the remainder of the winter and spring. To increase the chances of a true succession of decorative plants through the whole winter it was recommended (in 1861) that as well as a succession of flowers on one plant, a succession of plants should be grown – each at a slightly different stage – increasing the expense even more.

Given that the above is merely a summary outline of the recommendations of *The Gardeners' Chronicle*, one can only hope that the perpetual's 'show' of blooms on a cold and murky winter's day provided sufficient recompense for the attention and money lavished on it for the rest of the year.

Certainly the range of colours available in the 'tree carnations', even at this early stage in their development, was considerable, including some colours which have often been claimed to have first been produced much later, but research indicates were actually already available in the nineteenth century. Self colours included crimson, scarlet, white and yellow, while two tones generally had white grounds with flaked markings of crimson, scarlet or purple. Some had markings of more than one colour, like the old 'bizarres' of the seventeenth- and eighteenth-century florists. The 'tree picotee' – where the markings were supposed to be confined around the edges of the petals – came in an even wider range with primrose, yellow, orange-yellow, fawn-coloured and pale-slate backgrounds with lilac, rose or scarlet margins. A few daring specimens crossed the line between the carnation and the picotee and in the words of *The Gardeners' Chronicle* it was hoped that 'such double-faced behaviour, reprehensible though it may be, will yet be judged leniently by the floral critics in consideration of other good qualities they possess'.

While *The Gardeners' Chronicle* was heralding the arrival, loss and rediscovery of the 'tree carnation' in England (where it was later to be confusingly renamed the perpetual carnation), the plant was busy extending its reach across the Atlantic where its showy 'everlasting' blooms appealed to an emerging nation with a taste for the big and the brash. Again it was the French who were responsible for the initial wave of the remontant. In 1852 Charles Marc, a French flower fancier living close to New York, privately cultivated a number of remontant carnations which he had imported directly from France. His jealous American neighbours accused him of trying to keep these secret, although the idea of a florist keeping a winning flower secret seems most unlikely, and one wonders if it was his stock of plants that he kept closely guarded rather than the knowledge of the flowers themselves. Just a few years later, in 1856, further French examples were brought over from Lyons by the nurseries of Messrs Dailledouze, Zeller and Garde, of Flatbush, Long Island, and Charles Marc's fellow florists could finally purchase their own plants and compete against him on equal terms. Two years later the rather unfortunately located and named Flatbush nursery started producing their own hybrid seedlings, rather than relying on French imports, using as their basis for these new plants the ironically named variety 'La Purité'. By 1869 the firm had 54 varieties of perpetual flowering carnations of their own listed. Competition stiffened through the 1870s as another Frenchman, M. Donati of Astoria, Long Island, introduced a yellow-ground variety named 'Victor Emmanuel', which took the American horticultural world by storm. The Flatbush nursery may have fallen by the wayside slightly as by the 1950s 'Victor Emmanuel' was claimed to be the ancestor of most of the perpetual flowering carnations then available.

Once a connection with France was no longer a necessity for obtaining perpetual plants, American breeders took up the challenge themselves and by the late 1890s New York and Massachusetts were the centres of a carnation mania that was said to rival the 'Tulip-mania' of seventeenth-century Holland, albeit on sounder financial footing. In East Massachusetts there were 65 growers of carnations in the late nineteenth century, with 53 of those in Tewksbury, the 'Carnation Capital of the World' as it was then known. Tewksbury was the venue of the American Carnation Society's annual 'New Varieties

Day', and hundreds of varieties would be registered, with nurserymen and showers coming from as far afield as California. A Mr John Thorpe of Queens, New York, was one of the first into the ring on the side of the nurserymen with a larger flowered cultivar. Thorpe raised a variety named 'Portia' which, he claimed, had a flower 4 inches across on a 2-ft stem – a shape which must surely have looked somewhat ungainly to the unbiased. The 'Portia' appears to have been an exception to Thorpe's otherwise rather businesslike namings, which included varieties such as 'Mr B. K. Bliss', 'James Y. Murkland', 'Charles Henderson' and 'E. G. Hill', the last named after a fellow carnation breeder based in Richmond, Indiana. Who, one wonders, could fall in love with a plant that never revealed its full name, only its initials, rather like a salesman who had left you his business card after the briefest of meetings? John Thorpe was perhaps not as hard-hearted as his namings suggest. When one of his employees, a Mr W. P. Simmons, left to found his own nursery, Thorpe kindly gave him seeds from his own stock, with which Simmons was able to raise the rather less abruptly named 'Daybreak', 'Tidal Wave' and 'Silver Spray'. 'Daybreak' eventually found its way onto the potting bench of one of the leading pioneers of American carnation breeding, Mr Peter Fisher, who, in the words of the great English carnation breeder Montagu Allwood, 'astonished the whole carnation world' by crossing it with 'Van Leeuwen' to produce the first truly year-round perpetual with large cerise serrated flowers 3.5 inches across. 'Honest Peter', as Fisher was widely known, decided that the stunning new plant should not linger in the nursery, lovingly tended by slow and secretive nurserymen as they had done in Lyons all those years ago, but in true American style should be put up for auction to the highest bidder in a blaze of publicity. Fearing himself far too honest and retiring for the task, Fisher promptly hired a Mr Galvin of Boston as his sales and publicity agent.

The first person to bid for the carnation was the Chicago million-aire Harlow N. Higginbottom, who had offered a mere $6,000 for the plant and the right to name it 'Higginbottom' – perhaps not a name that would carry the new carnation with aplomb across the world. For whatever reason Mr Galvin declined the offer. The next approach to Galvin was an offer of $15,000 from a New York florist, but still 'Honest Peter' and his agent felt that more could be gained. Finally, in January 1899 Mr Galvin released to the press the news of the sale of Peter Fisher's new carnation to the American copper magnate and businessman Mr Thomas William Lawson for $30,000. Lawson (1857–1925), whose dreamlike Dreamwold estate in Massachusetts was financed through his manipulations of stock markets, immediately named the new variety after his wife ('Mrs T. W. Lawson') and declared that it would henceforth only be seen in the public gardens of the city of Boston, its exclusivity to that city being one of the conditions of sale.

Mr Lawson may have been moved by romance to name 'Mrs T. W. Lawson', but his financial acumen led him to hold the monopoly on the flower for a planned ten to fifteen years, with a profit of $2 for every dozen grown and an estimated fifty dozen being grown every day. From a handful of plants in early 1898, there were 8,000 in early 1899, each and every one the property of Mr Lawson, although still expertly and lovingly dealt with by the agent Mr Galvin. 'Mrs T. W. Lawson' became a fashion – every florist, every gardener and every lady with a corsage to wear demanded the flower, and profits literally bloomed. Despite the exclusivity placed on the variety, Lawson might also have taken the liberty of planting it in the flower beds of his Dreamwold home where it could keep company with the 'Dorothy Perkins' roses shown in postcards of the estate, along with the rather strange dovecote and striking water tower disguised as a German shingled tower complete with clock and bells (known locally as Lawson's Tower). The sturdy pink carnation would have matched well with the delicate ruffles of the ladylike 'Dorothy Perkins', itself named after the granddaughter of the American rose breeder Mr Charles Perkins in 1901. Rosa 'Dorothy Perkins' was held to be such a feminine bloom and to have such a delightful name that it was also used for a chain of dress shops most fashionable through the 1960s and '70s. Somehow 'Mrs T. W. Lawson' did not have quite the same ring, however beautiful the bloom.

The story of Thomas William Lawson does not have a happy ending. One fateful Friday 13th, a merchant ship he had invested in foundered at sea and with it so did his fortune. The ship which foundered was also called the Thomas W. Lawson, and she was wrecked off the Isles of Scilly at 2.30 am GMT on Saturday 14 December 1907 (but to Lawson, at home in Boston, it was at that time still Friday the 13th). The dream was gone and Dreamwold was sold. Mrs Lawson, whose actual name was Jeannie (she took the initials T. W. from her husband, as all good wives did in those far-off years), died in 1906, but the carnation that took her name went on to found its own 'empire', as famous in its own way as any dress shop. However, it needed a helping hand to do so, which takes us back again to the year 'Mrs T. W. Lawson' was first released.

At the Chicago exhibition of the American Carnation Society in that year a San Francisco breeder, John H. Sievers, had released samples of a new variety which he named 'Hannah Hobert'. Described as having 'larger and finer flowers' than anything the society had seen before, the 'Hannah Hobert' had a flower head measuring

Dreamwold, the residence of T. W. Lawson and his carnation.

Perpetual carnations grown commercially in an American greenhouse.

4.5 inches, as opposed to the mere 3.5 inches of its rival 'Mrs T. W. Lawson' – and yes, size does matter in the carnation world. The problem was that the distance from San Francisco to Chicago was such that the required fifty mature blooms could not be transported to the Chicago exhibition and so Mr Sievers had to be content with tantalizing the Carnation Society judges with just a few choice blooms. The secretary of the society had, however, taken cuttings – with permission of Mr Sievers – and had grown his own plants of 'Hannah Hobert', in the words of the *San Francisco Call* newspaper, 'out East'. His aim was to ready the flowers in time for the Philadelphia Exhibition of spring 1899, where he expected them to sweep the board, but in the event his plants were unnecessary. After the *San Francisco Call* had previewed the 'Mrs T. W. Lawson' vs 'Hannah Hobert' carnation competition it turned into a 'celebrity fight' with the *Pacific Rural Press* taking up the story. A wager of $5,000 was placed by Mr Lawson that no flower would beat 'Mrs T. W. Lawson' in a fair competition before 1 February 1900; suddenly Sievers leapt into action. Fifty specimens were sent express direct from the California nursery to the Philadelphia show, each in an individual glass tube inside a tin case with Californian water – with strict specifications that the water should not be changed during transportation for fear the carnations would not take to 'Eastern' water. After a tense judging 'Hannah Hobert' was awarded 86 points out of a possible 100, beating 'Mrs T. W. Lawson' into second place, and was therefore duly hailed by the *Pacific Rural Press* as the 'Californian Carnation'. Whether Mr Lawson paid Mr Sievers his $5,000 under the terms of the wager is sadly unrecorded.

Unlike with the rapid sale by 'Honest Peter' of 'Mrs T. W. Lawson', Mr Sievers was not in the market to sell the winning 'Hannah Hobert', even when pressed by the *San Francisco Call* reporter on whether he would take $30,000, the price 'Mrs T. W. Lawson' had reached. Sievers did, however, have a carnation that he hoped to sell instead, the rather dowdily named 'Ethel Crocker'. Ethel Crocker herself was a wealthy patron of the arts, including French Impressionism and classical music, both of which she promoted in California where her husband, William Crocker, was president of the Crocker National Bank and a prominent Republican. According to Mr Sievers, the carnation he had named after her would be worth every dollar of the more than $30,000 he was asking for! The development of cultivars by now gripped the newspaper-reading public and Mr Sievers treated the journalist from the *San Francisco Call* to a long disquisition on the breeding of carnations, using the analogies of weddings and divorces and describing the removal of anthers and introduction of pollen from other plants and the degeneration resulting from inbreeding within families. Producing a perfect mauve seedling from his collection for the benefit of the newspaper journalist, Sievers went on to describe how these rarely came true to colour and were poor fare for those looking to future generations, and as no more was heard of the perfect mauve carnation for many decades his prophecy was fulfilled. 'Hannah Hobert', however, with its fine bearing, perfect deep pink colour, perfume and strong head, was ideal for the marriage market. By now the religious doubts and uncertainties that had betrayed its seventeenth- and eighteenth-century forebears had been swept away and the production of different varieties and cultivars, whether by cross-pollination or by selection, was looked upon as the height of skill of a nurseryman. Sexuality of plants was taken for granted and by the mid-twentieth century one breeder even referred to an unsuccessful cultivar as being 'useless at stud' – providing an involuntary vision of the carnation in a rather more carnate form.

Having travelled first from France to both England and America, the next journey in the tangled history of the perpetual carnation was made from America to England. After several false starts in England, the enthusiasm of *The Gardeners' Chronicle* in 1861 for the perpetual might be thought to have reflected a more general taking up of the plant with a view to its improvement. Instead, many plants were matched with traditional English border carnations, forming a retrograde alliance which produced plants neither perpetual nor with the proper form of the tree carnation. The exceptions were two varieties – 'Miss Joliffe' (an old English pink variety) and 'Winter Cheer', rumoured to have contributed to the best American cultivars. It was from these two that the carnation descent proceeded. Released from its Boston imprisonment by the death of Mr Lawson, 'Mrs T. W. Lawson' was finally imported into England to great fanfare – before being promptly rejected by the Royal Horticultural Society as being unworthy of recognition owing to its unkempt flower and indented edges. Neatness was everything to the English carnation breeder. Petals, they declared, should be round-edged, even if this requirement led to show carnations lacking in size, flower numbers and scent. Size, they intoned, may impress in America, but in England neatness was all. In turn the English perpetual 'Miss Joliffe' had a similarly frosty reception on its first arrival in America, where the smallness of flower was her downfall.

At this stage (the early twentieth century) things became rather hazy and downright incestuous in the world of the carnation, as the French and English cultivars that had contributed early on to the development of the American perpetuals were bred back with them once they reached European shores. Most notably 'Mrs T. W. Lawson'

Brothers George and Montagu Allwood in the garden of their
cottage at Wivelsfield Green, Sussex, 1949.

was induced to breed with the English cultivar 'Winter Cheer', itself
a descendant of a French remontant, and most probably already
lurking in some form in the Lawson make-up. This resulted, among
others, in the variety patriotically and popularly named 'Britannia',
although in reality it was a disappointing pale silvery pink rather than
the red, white and blue one might hope for. 'Britannia', combining as
she did elements of the best of French, English and American carnations, perhaps with a smattering of central and southern Europe
from the dianthus' original homeland, ironically played a key role in
the development of one of the most popular traditional English

carnations, 'Wivelsfield White'. Which brings us rather nicely to the Allwoods.

Thanks to the three Allwood brothers, Montagu, George and Edward, the small village of Wivelsfield, lying on the northern edges of the chalky South Downs, became home to the largest ever nursery of carnations and pinks in England. So numerous were their employees (more than two hundred at the height of the nursery) that when the nursery closed at the end of the day women would call their children in from the streets for fear of them being knocked down by the mass of bicycling carnation growers intent on getting home for tea. In addition to this stream of bicycles, a stream of award-winning carnations emerged that challenged the supremacy of the American 'perpetual'. The Allwood brothers were born in Ludford, Lincolnshire, from a farming background. George Allwood had worked in carnation production in America and knew the latest techniques, the newest greenhouse designs and, of course, the latest cultivars and varieties, including the new strain of American 'tree carnations'. Montagu Allwood (1880–1958) was the gardener and horticulturalist, having worked his way up from 'crock boy' to become a 'humble plodding worker' in another large carnation firm in England. Edward Allwood had amassed some capital, which the brothers used to set up their own nursery, having worked outside of the garden and plant world in brewing. Montagu, the 'gardener', was to become the unexpected hit of the firm, a born showman and a superb salesman.

Purchasing land in Sussex rather than their homeland of Lincolnshire, both for the quality of light and length of day (vital in the raising of perpetual carnations) and also because the land was cheaper in Sussex, being of poorer agricultural quality, the Allwood Brothers founded their nursery in 1910. They acquired a 4-acre field for £344 and erected a 50-ft-span greenhouse, initially going into production with American tree carnations for the cut-flower trade. By 1912 they were exhibiting at the International Horticultural Exhibition at the Royal Hospital, Chelsea (later to become the preserve of the RHS and now commonly known as the Chelsea Flower Show), and by 1915 they were providing a postal service sending bouquets and button-holes across the country, despite the outbreak of war in 1914. Montagu C. Allwood ('Mont') soon became the frontman for the nursery and a well-known 'character' at flower shows and exhibitions. Every year he would present the queen with a small posy of carnations, and buttonholes were sent to the male members of the royal household, advertising not only the flowers themselves but the flowers-by-post service that the Allwoods had founded early on. When Chelsea's heavy canvas marquee blocked out too much light one year, causing all the carnations on the Allwood stand to loose their heady scent, his staff were instructed to wear a carnation-based scent to supplement the feeble perfume of the flowers.

Having established the nursery with the aim of developing per-petual flowering and 'tree' carnations and outdoing the Americans at their own game, the commercial breakthrough for the nursery actually came with the development of the 'Allwoodii' border pink just after the end of the First World War. A hybrid of the old-fashioned garden pink and the perpetual flowering carnation, the *Dianthus x Allwoodii* – the result of nine long years of trial and error – is everything one could ask for in a border plant: hardy, long-flowering, compact, often highly scented and suitable as a small cutting flower. As long as it has a well-drained soil, the *Dianthus x Allwoodii* will grow in borders, on sloping banks and rockeries, in window boxes, hanging baskets and of course in pots. There are even alpine varieties for the small trough garden. During the 1920s and '30s, the Allwoods had a contract to sell their potted pinks direct through Woolworths stores, then the most popular outlet for seeds and plants for suburban gardens. In an era when plants came as bare rooted or as seeds, this was revolutionary, and pre-dated by decades the invention of the 'garden centre' with its appeal of 'instant gar-dens' for the masses. The 1930s boom in new suburban housing, each with their own small front gardens ideal for bedding pinks, and the fall in price of the amateur's glasshouse, equally ideal for the perpetual flowering carnation, contributed to the phenomenal success of the company and its expansion to bolster the economies of other small Sussex villages such as Clayton, Burgess Hill, Henfield and later Hassocks.

Many of the women of those villages must have shared names with the pinks and carnations that employed their fathers and husbands. Montagu Allwood preferred to give his plants female names, hoping to encourage sales by their delicate feminine touch. The first of the Allwoodii pinks was named 'Mary' and became the parent plant of such varieties as 'Susan' (pale lilac-mauve), 'Eleanor' and, breaking the mould, 'Arthur'. It was, however, 'Doris', a semi-double pink with a raspberry-red eye, that was to become the most popular of all garden pinks. Montagu originally rejected it for being too similar to another cultivar, and almost consigned it to the compost heap, but one of the foremen thought it worth saving and carried on growing it in the nursery. Montagu fell in love at second sight, saying it was the best pink he had ever seen and when he launched it in 1945 he named it after his wife. His timing was immaculate, as suburban gardeners throughout England raced to re-stock their gardens devastated by five years of war and the 'Dig for Victory' campaign. Unfortunately, names go in and out of fashion and 'Doris', 'Edna' and 'Freda' no longer conjure up images of delicate, freshly scented young women, but perhaps their time will come again.

As war came and went, the patriotically named 'Blenheim', 'Spitfire' and 'Sunderland' carnations mixed with 'Wivelsfield White' (bred from the 'Britannia') and 'Wivelsfield Crimson', exporting both the carnations and the name of the small Sussex village back across the seas, whence the first wave of perpetual carnations had come. Nestling alongside carnations in the Allwood nurseries during the war were the peas, beans and cauliflowers that produced seed for the 'Dig for Victory' campaign, as each nursery came under government regulations to cut back non-productive plants and replace them with food that would win the war. With permanent nursery stocks limited to

overleaf: In many countries modern carnation growing has changed little over the decades.

10 per cent of the area of any company, and areas for decorative plants under glass or in the outside grounds severely limited (even for plants to be sold that year), many nurseries struggled during the war years. The Allwood brothers, however, rose above it all in a wave of patriotism that saw the strapline 'Allwood Brothers, Food Growers' appended to advertisements for everything from Allwoods' 'Prolific' peas, to onion seedlings, and even buckwheat for growing as hen feed. Every advert also included reference to the famous 'pinks', and in May 1943, when life was at its most difficult for many a gardener, you could still purchase a collection of dianthus seedlings in 'Four Varieties of Rainbow Loveliness' to cheer yourself and your garden up. Border carnations and pinks were among the most popular of wartime garden plants. During the Blitz the wartime radio broadcaster Cecil Middleton finished an edition of his popular *In Your Garden* with the comment on carnations that 'Some of you may find them difficult subjects, but it is because they like a lot of lime, so cheer up. The way things are going at the moment there will soon be plenty of mortar rubble about.' Middleton was admonished for his unscripted remark which the authorities felt might lower morale at home and give away to the Germans the damage their bombs were doing. Despite the

The 1936 Ideal Home Exhibition Carnation Garden by Allwood Bros.

'Supplement to " Amateur Gardening," June 25, 1938.

SOME HYBRIDS OF THE PINK FAMILY
Top—Examples of Sweet Wivelsfield ; left—The New Blue Dianthus ; right—Mule Pinks
(Natural Order, Caryophyllaceæ, Carnation Family)

Selection of Pinks including 'Sweet Wivelsfield'. *Amateur Gardening*. 25 June 1938.

damage wrought by the war to nursery stocks and skilled labour, by the 1950s you could complete the rainbow with the new hybrid *Dianthus x Allwoodii* 'Yellowhammer', the first truly yellow pink, which the nurseries had been working on for years to perfect.

Despite dividing his time between the nursery and the various shows and social events of the carnation world, Montagu Allwood

A wartime advertisement for Allwood Bros' pinks and vegetables.

also found time to write books and articles on the cultivation of the carnation, including snippets of history on the development of the various older varieties as well as detail on the modern cultivars. In the preface to his 1912 book *The Perpetual Flowering Carnation* (which also contained a piece by his brother George on the 'American System of Carnation Culture'), 'Mont' declared, 'I claim to be only a practical man, devoid of literary skill, and have been compelled to write the major portion of this book after twelve hours daily of hard work.' His ambitions were to be a 'good gardener' rather than a 'literary man', but the perpetual carnation was so popular that his book went to at least three editions in 1912, 1917 and 1920 – the last with an additional section dedicated to the Allwoodii. In the 1920s the upmarket periodical *Country Life* took up the baton of the carnation and asked Montagu to write a further book, rather ironically titled *Carnations for Every Garden and Greenhouse* (1926), later republished by the Allwood nursery itself as *Carnations and all Dianthus* (1936), and then *Carnations, Pinks and all Dianthus* (1947 and 1954). Following the editions maps the story of the differing varieties as their names appear for the first time, and also maps the life of Montagu himself. In 1940 'Mont' filled in the gaps left by the work on dianthus, and published an autobiography of reminiscences and reflections on his life. His work gives an insight into a man whose early years spanned the Edwardian era with its armies of gardeners and country house staff, and who now found himself on the eve of a changed world where flowers were flown around the world and home costs were so high that labour was being laid off. The book also provided a valuable history on the development of the Allwood nursery in its first three decades. In 1947, perhaps influenced by the changes wrought by the war and its aftermath, Montagu Allwood branched out to write a book, *English Countryside and Gardens*, in praise of times past and of plants future, while his final published work, *The Nobodies who Weave the Fabric of Civilisation*, was a heartfelt social history extolling the role of the husbandman, the horticulturalist and the land in a fast-changing and increasingly mechanized world.

Montagu Allwood died in 1958, aged 78, having spent 63 years in horticulture. Bereft of its 'showman', the Allwoods' nursery went into receivership within two years. Determined not to see the close of an era, a partnership was formed by ex-Allwood employees so that the varieties lovingly created and named could be continued. In 1994 new buyers were found who, although not from the Allwood family, came from 'nursery stock'. Having celebrated its centenary in 2010, Allwoods is still a family-run firm with over four hundred varieties of dianthus, including many of those developed by the original brothers in the early twentieth century. By 2012 part of the Allwood production was moved to Cheam, Surrey, but part remained at Hassocks in West Sussex, just 6 miles from Wivelsfield, and 600 miles from that small nursery in Lyons where it all began.

Epilogue: The Everlasting Carnation

❧

I n 1996, against a backdrop of global disagreement on the role of genetic modification in foodstuffs, the company Florigene unveiled a mauve carnation named 'Moondust'. 'Moondust' was the end result of a series of developments that had started five years earlier with the isolation of the gene responsible for blue pigmentation in flowers. Anxious to capture some of the extraordinary wealth of the world's cut flower market, estimated to be worth u.s. $30 billion annually, Florigene aimed to produce not only a blue and blue-mauve carnation, but roses and chrysanthemums in the same shade. Creation of these colours by genetic modification would enable Florigene to command enhanced prices for their products, which they predicted would place them at the top end of the flower market. With the carnation trade alone worth $10 billion a year, it was a market worth aiming for. Using patents to protect its investment in the u.s., Europe, Japan and Australia, the company aimed to accomplish the same sort of monopoly as the American businessman Mr T. W. Lawson had imposed on the carnation he had named in honour of his wife in 1895. The carnation and the rose, with the natural range of reds, pinks and occasional yellows and tawnys, naturally carry the pigments of flavonoids and carotenoids, which produce those colours. Getting technical, as bioscientists have to do, flavonoids can be broken down further into those which produce pinks and reds and those which produce blue. It is the blue shade, the delphinidin pigment, that is never found naturally

Growing dianthus under cover in a modern polytunnel
still creates an uplifting show of colour.

in roses or carnations, which only have cyanidin and pelargonidin. By isolating the delphinidin from a petunia and transferring it to a carnation, Florigene accomplished in five years what nurserymen and florists had been attempting for five centuries.

What Florigene did next was even more astonishing: they gave their blue carnation 'everlasting' life. After isolating and blocking the hormone that induces the flowers to age and wither, they produced genetically modified plants that did not age. With international trade in carnations being carried out from Australia to Japan, from Israel and South America to North America, and from the Netherlands across Europe, the ability to maintain a long life with little change in appearance has obvious advantages. What the flower industry term 'long vase life' has always been a feature of the carnation, but ageing can now be slowed almost infinitely, at least over the time period one might expect to keep a bouquet. Disease resistance was added into the mix in the following years to create an almost invincible plant, now available in shades of blue, lavender and purple. With genetic patents and licences in place across much of the world, the exotically coloured and enviably ever-youthful carnation is a man-made incarnation of the original divine flower: a flower that has played its role in religion, art and culture and is now at the forefront of molecular science and the moral debate that surrounds it.

An Explication of Carnation
Types and Common Terms
❧

> There are at this day under the name of Caryophyllus comprehended
> diverse and sundrie sorts of plants, of such variable colours, and also severall
> shapes, that a great and large volume would not suffice to write of every one
> JOHN GERARD, *The Herball, or General Historie of Plants* (1597)

For the dianthus novice, the multiple terms and names given to different colourings, markings and types of carnation and pink can be mystifying. In addition, these terms have themselves often changed over time, particularly in nursery descriptions of show categories. Where an early nineteenth-century florist might divide his collections into bizarres, flakes and picotees, a twentieth-century grower might discuss perpetuals and malmaisons, while pinks sometimes take the terminology of their more forthright carnation cousins but can also revel in names of their own. The exact colouring and markings described by such terms, or desired by the florists using them, have also changed over the years such that those held to be perfect in one period might be undesirable at another. The following attempts to bring some simplification and order for the general reader, although variation over time and between countries must be accepted.

BIZARRE: a class of carnation with a white background and a series of longitudinal stripes usually of two colours, sometimes three. Hence 'scarlet bizarres' have scarlet and maroon stripes, 'pink bizarres' have pink and purple stripes and so on. At some periods the 'bizarre' was

Birthday Greeting.

May Grace and Truth
thy life surround,
And Peace thro' all thy
days abound!

also permitted spots. The term 'bizarre' is most usually met with in
older works on carnations and may also be spelt 'bizard'.

BORDER CARNATION: hardy carnations which may be grown outside,
literally 'in the flower border'. The various types of 'florists' flower
(see BIZARRES, FLAKES and FANCIES) were often grown in the border
but usually with protection and most writers agreed that even border
carnations benefited from being started in pots.

BURSTER: the term used for some of the early large flowered carnations, such as malmaison, when the calyx frequently split open prior
to the flower blooming. The opposite of the burster was the 'whole
blower' and florists' shows often specified whether bursters or only
whole blowers would be accepted in an exhibition class.

The 'Bizarre' or 'bizard' carnation in variegated crimson and scarlet versions, as approved and described by James Maddox in *The Florist's Directory* (1810).

CHINESE (orCHINA) PINK: *Dianthus sinensis* (also or originally *D. chinensis* in some works). An annual or biennial garden pink. Confusingly originally referred to as the 'Indian Pink' when seeds were first sent from China to France in the eighteenth century.

FANCY: another older term (along with BIZARRE and FLAKE). Fancies were a carnation with a wide range of colours irregularly marked on a white, cream, apricot or yellow [back]ground. In Germany these were also known as bizarres. The fancy was also referred to as the 'fantasy' in France, where some held them in low regard.

FLAKE: flakes, along with BIZARRES, were the most beloved by florists in the early centuries of carnation cultivation in England. In the seventeenth century it was said by florist and botanist John Rae that 'selfs were little esteemed but those flowers are chiefly valued which are well flaked, striped or powdered'. With a white or cream [back]ground, unlike the bizarre, flakes have stripes of a single colour, typically scarlet, purple or rose/pink with the stripes going the whole length of the petal.

FLAMAND: a type of PINK favoured in France in the nineteenth century, which has perfectly rounded petals with three colours 'longitudinally'. Fifty varieties were known and said to be rare and ancient in origin. The carnation lover the Baron de Ponsort contrasted it with the 'detestable fashionable "Fantasies"' produced by the florists of England which he regarded as morally degenerate.

LACED PINK: also known as Scotch Pinks due to their popularity in Scotland, in particular among the cloth weavers of Paisley. Laced pinks should be divided into three sections with a white or rose ground, a dark 'eye' and laced edge.

MALMAISON (AND PERPETUAL MALMAISON): originating in France in the 1850s, the malmaison was classified by the end of the nineteenth century as a type of TREE CARNATION. They were commonly used for buttonholes and were fashionable in the Edwardian era. The 'perpetual malmaison' is variously thought to have been either a well-scented perpetual or a cross with a malmaison.

MARGUERITE: a group of carnations with clove-scented flowers and fringed petals, producing flowers freely but with the disadvantage that they do not last long once cut.

MULE: a hybrid between two species that cannot go on to reproduce itself by seed.

PAINTED LADY: a carnation or pink with the underside of the petal white and the upper-side red, pink or purple as if painted, the colour sometimes concentrated in the centre. These were a show class at some period, but appear to have become neglected in the nineteenth century.

PANACH'T (OR PANACHED): according to John Evelyn (1693), the term for a tulip or carnation when they are 'curiously striped, and diversified with several Colours like a gaudy Plume of Feathers'. By the mid-eighteenth century this had been replaced by flaked or FLAKE and BIZARRE.

PERPETUAL CARNATION: developed in France in around 1842 and then in both America and England in the 1860s, the perpetual carnation flowers over a greatly extended period of the year – therefore it was originally not truly 'perpetual'. Some cultivars also possess large blooms. The perpetual carnation is primarily a glasshouse carnation in use for bouquets and so on.

PHEASANT EYE PINK: a class found in early nineteenth-century American seed catalogues. This name was used for a vast group of pinks that evolved in Britain by the late seventeenth century and were characterized by flowers marked with a dark central blotch and a soft irregular band of colour along the jagged margin of each petal. In the smooth-petalled form these were included within the LACED type in England.

PICOTEE: from the French *piquotée* and *picoté*. A type of carnation with narrow or broad rounded petals bordered with a band of colour at the margin. The ground colour of yellow was originally highly sought after. For exhibition purposes they may be further divided according to the colour and the heaviness of the marking. In addition a 'yellow-ground' picotee was much sought after in the nineteenth century. William Robinson (in *The English Flower Gardener*) claims that picotees should be dusted with spots but this does not agree with earlier definitions that state that any spotting would be a drawback. An 'edged' flower is first mentioned in *The Florist's Vade-Mecum* in 1683 but early examples still had serrated-edged petals.

PINK: a different species to the carnation (*Dianthus caryophyllus*), the garden pink is an improved form of *Dianthus plumarius*, although hybridization with others including *Dianthus superbus* (the fringed pink) has also produced, for example, *Dianthus x Allwoodii* and a range of other species and cultivars from the original.

REMONTANT CARNATION: from the French for 'repeat flowering', the remontant carnation may have appeared in France as early as the mid-eighteenth century under the title of 'carnation Mayonnais', but was not fully recognized until around 1830 when it contributed to the development of the perpetual carnation.

SELF: depending on when the term is being used, either a single-colour carnation, a pink one, or one where any marking has a very similar colour to the background.

SPRAY CARNATION: American strain of year-round flowering carnations with several blooms on each stem, originating in the mid-twentieth century. See also TREE CARNATION.

TREE CARNATION: originally (in the mid- to late nineteenth century) an alternative name for the PERPETUAL CARNATION, and particularly used in America. It came into use again for the new strains of American carnations produced in the 1950s and '60s. These are true year-round carnations, unlike most perpetuals. They also have several flowers on each stem, giving rise to their alternative name, 'spray carnation'.

Timeline

❧

2nd century BC	Image of a wild carnation on the walls of the House of the Faun, Pompeii
c. 1270	*Dianthus caryophyllus*, the true carnation, thought to arrive in Europe, probably from Tunisia
1460	Spanish recorded growing 'carnations' near Valencia, giving rise to the name 'Spanish gilliflower', used in some English herbals
1470s	The first record of the *oeillet* in France
c. 1475	Introduction of the carnation, *Dianthus caryophyllus*, to northern Europe
1506–7	Raphael paints *Madonna of the Pinks*, using the flower as a symbol for love and divinity
1587	First yellow carnation recorded in England by John Gerard, having been sent from Poland
1632	Mistress Tuggie of Westminster becomes famous for her 'gilleflowers', including 'Master Tuggie's Princess'
1665	John Rae lists 91 varieties of carnation in his book on flowers; by 1685 more than 360 different forms were known
1676	Mention of gilliflowers and clove gilliflowers occurs in America as early as 1676 in Thomas Glover's *An Account of Virginia*, where he notes 'clove-gilliflowers' in planters' gardens

1687	Seeds of the 'China Pink' (*Dianthus chinensis*), also known as the 'Indian Pink', brought from China to France
1719	Double-flowered China pinks recorded in Paris
1720	Thomas Fairchild creates his hybrid 'mule' between a *Dianthus barbatus* and a *Dianthus caryophyllus*, inadvertently challenging God's role in creation
1786–1807	On a list of plants sent to Francis Eppes around 1786, the American president, Thomas Jefferson, includes 'Giroffle royal. Gilly flowers, royal. to be sown in March. very fine & very rare'. At Monticello, Thomas Jefferson sowed China pinks, which he acquired from Philadelphia nurseryman Bernard McMahon in 1807
c. 1792	Acceptance of the pink as a florists' flower in England
1820	Publication of Thomas Hogg's book on the cultivation and showing of florists' flowers, including the carnation and the pink
1830	Introduction of the buttonhole in coats, allowing the creation of the boutonnière, of which the red and white carnation were the most popular
c. 1857	Creation of the malmaison carnation in France
1868	Introduction of *Dianthus* 'Mrs Sinkins' by Charles Turner, Slough nurseryman. Bred by Mr Sinkins, superintendent of Slough Workhouse, and named after his wife. Perhaps the most famous of all pinks
1885–7	John Singer Sargent paints *Carnation, Lily, Lily, Rose*
1891	Founding of the American Carnation Society
1892	Opening night of *Lady Windermere's Fan* and the wearing of the green carnation by Oscar Wilde and his followers
1895	Creation of the cultivar 'Mrs T. W. Lawson', which would revolutionize the American 'tree' carnation and eventually the English perpetual carnation

1901	Assassination of William McKinley, 25th president of the United States, shortly after he gave away his lucky carnation
1910	Founding of the Allwood nursery, Sussex, which went on to breed the Allwoodii strain of pinks and carnations, securing the dianthus as one of the most popular garden plants of the early twentieth century
1917	7 November: Russian Revolution, commemorated annually ever since with red carnations
1920	Creation of a Carnation Garden at the Ideal Home Exhibition (London)
1965	Release of a Russian postage stamp featuring the red carnation of socialism
1974	The Carnation Revolution in Portugal, a military coup against the right-wing regime where carnations were placed in gun barrels
1991–6	Isolation of the blue pigmentation in flowers by the company Florigene leads to the creation of a true blue carnation. Using genetic modifications Florigene also removes the hormone ethylene, which causes decay, increasing the shelf life of the carnation and allowing reliable exports of 'fresh' flowers between Australia and Japan, and from flower growers in Israel and the Netherlands

References
❧

1 The Divine Flower

1 *Dianthus inodorus* (now *Dianthus sylvestris*), identified by the Flemish botanist Matthias de l'Obel (1538–1616).
2 W. Jashemski and F. Meyer, eds, *The Natural History of Pompeii* (Cambridge, 2002), p. 108.
3 Steven Bailey, *Carnations, Perpetual-flowering Carnations, Borders and Pinks* (London, 1990).
4 A. Hill, 'Henry Nicholson Ellacombe (1822–1916), Canon of Bristol, Vicar of Bitton and Rural Dean: A Memoir', *Country Life* (1919), p. 74.
5 Ibid.
6 Ibid., p. 131.
7 Bailey, *Carnations*, p. 175; Eleanour Sinclair Rohde, *The Story of the Garden* (London, 1932), p. 42.
8 Johannes Ruellius, or Jean Ruel, or Jean de la Ruelle (1474–1537) was a French botanist and physician whose main work was his 1536 *De natura stirpium*, a treatise on botany based on the classical sources, using the same style and format.
9 Bailey, *Carnations*, p. 175.
10 Baron de Ponsort, *Monographie du Genre Oeillet et principalement de l'œillet flammand*, 2nd edn (Paris, 1844).
11 The list of flavourings includes liquorice, zedoary, nutmeg and cetewale. Zedoary has a root like ginger and was used in ale. From A. Mayhew and W. Skeat, *A Concise Dictionary of Middle English: From AD 1150 to 1580* (London, 1888).
12 Penelope Hobhouse, *Plants in Garden History* (London, 1997), p. 75.
13 *La Teseida*, Boccaccio Cod 2617 fol. 53 (Osterreichisches Nationalbibliothek, Vienna).
14 British Library Ms Add 38126 f.110.
15 Rohde, *The Story of the Garden*, p. 125.
16 *Virgin and Child*, c. 1490, Dieric Bouts, Capilla Real, Granada/Scala.
17 Lucia Impelluso, *Nature and Its Symbols* (Los Angeles, CA, 2003), p. 115.
18 Ibid.

19 William Turner, *A New Herball* (London, 1551–68).
20 Jan van Eyck, *Portrait of a Man with Carnation*, c. 1463, Kunsthistorisches Museum, Vienna.
21 Hans Memling, *Portrait of a Man with a Pink Carnation*, c. 1475, The Morgan Library and Museum, New York.
22 Michael Ostendorfer, *Self-portrait*, c. 1520, Liechtenstein Museum, Vienna.
23 Rembrandt, *Portrait of a Woman with a Pink*, early 1660s, Metropolitan Museum of Art, New York.
24 Alice M. Coats, *The Treasury of Flowers* (London, 1975), p. 4.
25 Rohde, *The Story of the Garden*, p. 54.
26 Hobhouse, *Plants in Garden History*, pp. 14–15.
27 Stefano Carboni, *Venice and the Islamic World 828–1797* (Paris, 2006), p. 296.

2 What's in a Name?

 1 Henry Lyte (1529–1607) translated the book from French (itself translated from Dutch) and added a few comments of his own plus new woodcut illustrations.
 2 Peggy Cornett, 'Pinks, Gilliflowers & Carnations – The Exalted Flowers', www.monticello.org, January 1998.
 3 Eleanour Sinclair Rohde, *The Story of the Garden* (London, 1932), p. 86.
 4 William Lawson, *A New Orchard and Garden with The Country Housewife's Garden* (London, 1618).
 5 Henry Lyte, *A New Herball* (London, 1578).
 6 Rohde, *The Story of the Garden*, p. 94.
 7 John Parkinson, *Paradisi in sole, paradisus terrestris* (London, 1629), pp. 308–11.
 8 Thomas Johnson, *Gerard's Herball, or General Historie of Plants*, revised and enlarged edn (London, 1633).
 9 Louis Boulanger, *Jardinage des Oeillets* (Paris, 1647).
10 John Rae (1627–1705) of Black Notley, near Braintree, Essex, was a botanist and zoologist, and one of the first in a long line of parson-naturalists and garden lovers. The upheavals of the mid-seventeenth century saw his political and religious beliefs fall in and out of favour, in common with Hanmer and Evelyn, and resulted in periods of semi-retirement.
11 Charles Ward, *The American Carnation* (New York, 1911), p. 18.
12 Penelope Hobhouse, *Plants in Garden History* (London, 1997), p. 113.
13 Sir Thomas Hanmer Bart, *The Garden Book of Sir Thomas Hanmer Bart*, intro. Eleanour Sinclair Rohde (London, 1933). The 1933 book was reprinted as a limited edition in 1991 by Clwyd County Council.
14 Murrey is a dark reddish purple – a sort of wine- or port-stain colour.
15 Rohde, *The Story of the Garden*, p. 158.
16 John Rae, *Flora or Complete Florilege* (London, 1665).
17 John Harvey in his examination of the plants in *Elysium Britannicum* has suggested that the plants mentioned were almost entirely those which

had entered the country or been developed here by 1660–85. See John Harvey, 'The Plants in John Evelyn's "Elysium Britannicum"', in Theresa O'Malley and J. Wolschke-Bulmahn, *John Evelyn's 'Elysium Britannicum'* (Washington, DC, 1998).

18 John Evelyn, *Elysium Britannicum or The Royal Gardens* [facsimile] (Philadelphia, PA, 2001).

19 Mathew Stevenson (fl. 1654–85), *Occasions Off-spring. Or, Poems Upon Severall Occasions.* This particular poem is entitled 'At the Florists Feast in Norwich: Flora Wearing a Crown'. There is no specific date for this collection.

20 A 'sport' in horticulture is an unexpected mutation on a part of the plant that makes it look different to the rest of the plant. Often these may be prized but a florist wanting to keep their varieties true will not welcome such change. Where they do contain desirable elements, such sports may be difficult to reproduce and often revert to their original form.

21 Thomas Hogg, *A Practical Treatise on the Culture of the Carnation, Pink, Auricula, Polyanthus, Ranunculus, Tulip, Hyacinth, Rose and Other Flowers*, 2nd edn (London, 1822).

22 See Chapter Five for the role of the French empress Joséphine de Beauharnais in the cultivation of the picotee.

3 Nature's Bastards: From Divinity to Blasphemy

1 Anon, *La Culture des fleurs*, quoted in Elizabeth Hyde, 'Flowers of Distinction: Taste, Class and Floriculture in Seventeenth-century France', in *Bourgeois and Aristocratic Cultural Encounters in Garden Art, 1550–1850*, ed. Michel Conan (Washington, DC, 2002), p. 87.

4 Florists, Weavers and Cottagers

1 Quoted in Ruth Duthie, *Florists' Flowers and Societies Shire Histories* (Aylesbury, 1988).

2 Ibid.

3 William Hanbury, *A Complete Body of Planting and Gardening. Containing the Natural History, Culture, and Management of Deciduous and Evergreen Forest-trees; . . . also Instructions for Laying-out and Disposing of Pleasure and Flower-gardens; including the Culture of Prize Flowers, Perennials, Annuals, Biennials, & c . . .*, vol. 1 (London, 1770).

4 Duthie, *Florists' Flowers and Societies Shire Histories.*

5 John Claudius Loudon, *An Encyclopaedia of Gardening* (London, 1829), p. 1089.

6 See 'William Morris and Wallpaper Design', at www.vam.ac.uk, accessed 1 April 2016.

5 Fit for Royalty: Empresses and Queens

1 Penelope Hobhouse, *Plants in Garden History* (London, 1997), p. 121.

2 In her 1957 book, *Herbs to Quicken the Senses*, Mrs C. F. Leyel appears
to give credit to Queen Henrietta Maria herself, but in his *Flora Historica*
of 1824 Henry Phillips merely declares that there were 49 varieties listed
by Gerard in the period of Charles I, 'whose Queen was excessively fond
of flowers'.

3 Jean de La Quintinie, *The compleat gard'ner, or, Directions for cultivating and right
ordering of fruit-gardens and kitchen-gardens with divers reflections on several parts of
husbandry, in six books: to which is added, his treatise of orange-trees, with the raising
of melons, omitted in the French editions*, trans. John Evelyn (London, 1693).

4 Hobhouse, *Plants in Garden History*, p. 180.

5 Thomas Hogg, *A Practical Treatise on the Culture of the Carnation, Pink, Auricula,
Polyanthus, Ranunculus, Tulip, Hyacinth, Rose and Other Flowers*, 6th edn
(London, 1839), p. 83.

6 H. Phillips, *Flora Historica or The Three Seasons of the British Parterre* (London,
1834), p. 54.

7 R. P. Brotherston, *The Book of the Carnation* (London, 1904).

8 Advertisement for Floris perfume, www.florislondon.com.

9 *The Gardener's Magazine and Register of Rural and Domestic Improvement*, VII
(1831), pp. 632–4.

10 Ibid., VIII (1832), p. 745.

11 Mr William Woollard died in 1852, leaving his property to his wife
Margaret. In 1854 the Royal William Inn was put up to let. *Suffolk Record
Office H88/1/959* and *Ipswich Journal* (27 May 1854).

12 Letter from William to George FitzClarence (his oldest illegitimate son),
21 March 1818, quoted in Philip Ziegler, *King William IV* (London, 1971),
p. 122.

13 In September 1838 an 18-ft-high tableau was created at the Royal
Salisbury and West of England Dahlia Society composed of 5,000 dahlia
flowers depicting the society's arms and motto, as well as the name of
Queen Adelaide and the two Vice-Patronesses Countess of Radnor
and Pembroke, *The Gardener's Magazine and Register of Rural and Domestic
Improvement*, XVI (1839), p. 683.

14 Steven Bailey, *Carnations* (London, 1982), p. 177.

15 T. H. Cook, James Douglas and J. F. McLeod, *Carnations & Pinks*
(New York, 1911), p. viii.

16 British Pathé News 1925, 'The Late Queen Alexandra'.

17 Sarah Tooley, *The Life of Queen Alexandra* (London, 1902).

18 Andrew Morton, *17 Carnations: The Windsors, the Nazis and the Cover Up*
(London, 2015).

19 Princess Louise d'Orléans (1812–1850), 'Carnation', Fitzwilliam
Museum, Cambridge, Object Number: PD.107-1973.9.

6 A Rainbow of Pinks

1 Baron de Ponsort, *Monographie du Genre Oeillet et principalement de l'œillet flammand*, 2nd edn (Paris, 1844), trans. Caroline Holmes (pers. comm.).
2 'Mirrors of Washington', *Wall Street Journal*, 26 September 1924.
3 Oscar Wilde quoted in the *Wall Street Journal*, 2 October 1894.
4 Noël Coward, in the *Noël Coward Diaries*, ed. S. Morley and G. Payn (London, 1982), p. 508.

7 A Picture of Pink

1 Edmund Gosse, quoted in The Hon. Evan Charteris, *John Sargent* (London, 1927), pp. 74–5.
2 Pierre-Joseph Redouté, *Choix de plus belles . . .* (Fruits and Flowers), ed. and intro. Eva Mannering (London, 1955).

8 A Strengthener of the Heart and Brain

1 Baron de Ponsort, *Monographie du Genre Oeillet et principalement de l'œillet flammand*, 2nd edn (Paris, 1844), trans. Caroline Holmes (pers. comm.).
2 Alice Coats, *Flowers and their Histories* (London, 1968).

Further Reading

The carnation world has a long history of books written for the interested amateur – many of which have been overtaken with time and new varieties and methods. Listed here are mainly works which cover the history of the carnation or have been published at seminal points in its development.

Allwood, Montagu, *Carnations, Pinks and All Dianthus*, 4th edn (Haywards Heath, Sussex, 1954)

Brotherston, R. P., *The Book of the Carnation* (London, 1904)

Coats, Alice, *Flowers and their Histories* (London, 1968)

Cook, T. H., James Douglas and J. F. McLeod, *Carnations and Pinks* (New York, 1911)

Duthie, Ruth, *Florists' Flowers and Societies* (Aylesbury, 1968)

Hichens, Robert Smythe, *The Green Carnation* (London, 1894)

Hobhouse, Penelope, *Plants in Garden History* (London, 1997)

Hogg, Thomas, *A Practical Treatise on the Culture of the Carnation, Pink, Auricula, Polyanthus, Ranunculus, Tulip, Hyacinth, Rose, and Other Flowers*, 2nd edn (London, 1822)

Impelluso, Lucia, *Nature and its Symbols* (Los Angeles, CA, 2003)

Leapman, Michael, *The Ingenious Mr Fairchild* (London, 2000)

Rohde, Eleanour Sinclair, *The Story of the Garden* (London, 1932)

Ward, Charles, *The American Carnation* (New York, 1911)

Willes, Margaret, *The Gardens of the British Working Class* (New Haven, CT, and London, 2014)

—, *The Making of the English Gardener: Plants, Books and Inspiration, 1560–1660* (New Haven, CT, and London, 2011)

Associations and Websites

ALLWOODS NURSERY
The oldest surviving carnation and pinks nursery, founded in 1910 by the Allwood brothers. They stock many heritage varieties of pinks including the original sops-in-wine, 'Pheasant Eye' (pre-1600s), 'Queen of Sheba' (seventeenth century), 'Fair Folly' (1700), 'Inchmery' (1800), 'Mrs Sinkins' (1868) as well as malmaison and their own 'Allwoodii' carnations and pinks
www.allwoods.net

BRITISH NATIONAL CARNATION SOCIETY
Yearbook, newsletters and show entries as well as advice on growing and finding old and new cultivars. Also affiliated local carnation societies
www.britishnationalcarnationsociety.co.uk

GRAVETYE MANOR
Country house and garden in Sussex, England, once owned by William Robinson, who championed cottage garden carnations and pinks. Now a fine hotel and restaurant with a restored garden
www.gravetyemanor.co.uk

GREAT NORTHERN CARNATION SOCIETY
Established in 1989. Yearbook, newsletters and show entries as well as advice on growing and showing
http://thegncs.co.uk

MALMAISON CARNATIONS
The national collection is held by Jim Marshall, who also raises plants for sale: Hullwood Barn, Shelley, Ipswich, Suffolk, England, IP7 5RE
jim@malmaisons.plus.com

MONTICELLO
The historic home of President Thomas Jefferson maintains his garden where he raised carnations and pinks. The site also includes research into the history of plants in America and the exchanges made between Jefferson and plant collectors such as Peter Collinson
www.monticello.org

THE SCOTTISH NATIONAL SWEET PEA, ROSE AND CARNATION SOCIETY
One of the oldest gardening societies in Scotland with members keeping and showing new and old varieties
www.snsprcs.org.uk

WHETMAN PINKS
Nursery established in 1936 for the breeding and supply of pinks
www.whetmanpinks.com

Acknowledgements

I would like to thank Michael Leaman of Reaktion Books for commissioning this book and allowing me the pleasure of exploring the history of the carnation and all the amazing stories that centre on it, and also for waiting patiently for its delayed completion. Amy Salter (Assistant Editor at Reaktion Books) was also unfailingly helpful and patient. My friend and garden historian colleague Caroline Holmes provided much-needed translations of the fervent and florid outpouring of the nineteenth-century Baron de Ponsort, and as ever guided me towards some other snippets of carnation folklore which I would otherwise have missed. Kathy Stevenson shared her knowledge of cooking with carnations and pinks, while Philip Norman of the Garden Museum (London) as ever produced a range of images that provided food for thought at an early stage in the book's genesis while Susannah Jayes took ideas for images forward.

Permissions

For permission to reproduce an excerpt from the poem 'The Old Jam Jar' © Harry J. Horsman, 2005. For permission to reproduce an excerpt from the poem 'Carnations in the Garden' © Gert Strydom.

For permission to quote the lyrics from 'Bitter Sweet' © NC Aventales AG, 1929 by permission of Alan Brodie Representation Ltd, www.alanbrodie.com.

Photo Acknowledgements

The author and the publishers wish to express their thanks to the below sources of illustrative material and/or permission to reproduce it.

AKG Images: pp. 14 (British Library), 16 (Mondadori Portfolio/Antonio Quattrone), 37 (British Library), 74 (Florilegius), 103 (bilwissedition), 116 (Sputnik), 139, 140 (Florilegius), 145 (IAM), 160 (Florilegius), 196 (Florilegius); Alamy: pp. 26 (Sonia Halliday), 113 (Photos 12), 117 bottom (dpa picture alliance); Courtesy of Allwoods: pp. 34, 97; author's private collection: pp. 20, 50, 52, 121, 122, 123, 124, 146, 152, 158, 163, 168, 176, 177, 186, 188, 195; © The Trustees of the British Museum, London: pp. 21, 27, 53, 65, 78, 80, 82, 153, 164; Getty Images: p. 180 (Picture Post); REX Shutterstock: p. 120 (Snap); Shutterstock: pp. 10 (ChWeiss), 11 (Bakusova), 23 (Bildagentur Zoonar GmbH), 30 (AlexanderZam), 55 (Lebendkulturen.de), 79 (reitory), 108–9 (petrovichlili), 117 top (EvrenKalinbacak), 127 (Melissa Fague), 144 (violeta pasat), 149 (Volkova), 155 (Kirayonak Yuliya), 184–5 (TanyaRusanova), 192 (lynea); Spitalfields Life/ The Gentle Author: p. 57; Victoria & Albert Museum, London: pp. 17, 22, 28, 61, 77, 84, 85.

Index